A Shared Condition

ALSO FROM THE VENICE COLLECTIVE

Angle of Reflection (Arctos Press, 2017)

A Shared Condition

Poetry from the Venice Collective

Marjorie Becker
Jeanette Clough
Dina Hardy
Paul Lieber
Sarah Maclay
Holaday Mason
Jim Natal
Jan Wesley
Brenda Yates
Mariano Zaro

MOON TIDE PRESS

~ 2025 ~

A Shared Condition: Poetry from the Venice Collective
All work Copyright © 2025 by individual authors: Marjorie Becker; Jeanette Clough; Dina Hardy; Paul Lieber; Sarah Maclay; Holaday Mason; Jim Natal; Jan Wesley; Brenda Yates; Mariano Zaro.

All rights reserved. No part of this book may be used or reproduced in any manner whatsoever without written permission from either the author or the publisher, except in the case of credited epigraphs or brief quotations embedded in articles or reviews.

Editor-in-chief
Eric Morago

Editor Emeritus
Michael Miller

Marketing Specialist
Ellen Webre

Proofreader
LeAnne Hunt

Cover Photographs
Marina Noir by Holaday Mason (front) & *Untitled* by Sarah Maclay (back).

Book design
ash good

Moon Tide logo design
Abraham Gomez

A Shared Condition: Poetry from the Venice Collective
is published by Moon Tide Press

Moon Tide Press
6709 Washington Ave. #9297
Whittier, CA 90608
www.moontidepress.com

FIRST EDITION

Printed in the United States of America

ISBN 978-1-957799-23-0

Contents

Preface: The Venice Collective   9

Marjorie Becker

The Inner Utter Other Ways to Stay, to Splay, to Rearrange the Silk and its Eternities in Satin and Survival Lust When Dozing There and Then Recall the Sense of Scenery, the Nonchalance Required to Cook, There and Then to Sense How Women Made it, Make it Still within the World of Happenstance and Brilliant Strokes upon the Riled-up Piano Keys of Being   11

Shad, Malomars   13

Encased, Ablaze with Gold   14

The Stash of Jewels Hiding Far Away Within the Purple Dense, the True Intense, So Come Around, the Ground Revives the Pawn Shop Near the River's Sight, its Succulence   15

Voices from the Macon Purple Pawn   16

When Diamonds Found the Ways Without, Within   17

Replete with Seers Singing Scheme, the Sapphire Light Itself Prepared a Theme, a Way to Wonder, Blunder, Ponder Flight as Generous as Porch Light When It Comes Around, Illuminates the Skies of Peace and Wild Prosperities Again, Again, Again, and Once Again   18

The Wingéd Wild Abides, Abides, Bestows, Endures Inside Predictions Spelling Out a Sense of Peace, a Way, a Splay, a Place Where Here We Sense We See, We Wing the Newest Naked Notion Placed Where Peace Itself Might Murmur, Shimmer, Settle   19

What We Didn't Do and What We Did   20

Pie Filling   21

Golden Feather Once Forlorn, Unborn, Adrift, Arrives Decides How Fate Can, There within the Purple Pawn Shop, Ponder Light, Abide	22
Restoration of Macon's Temple after the 2023 Fascist Attack	23
They Bought My Time So Cheaply	24
Summer Fruit	25
How We Orchestrated Macon in the Wild	26

Jeanette Clough

Unknown	28
Imagining the Desert Trumpet	30
Silver Reef	31
Insects in the Desert	33
Moth	34
The Jasmine Corridor	35
Heist	36
Evocation (Streets)	37
Ardor	38
Incognito	39
Pillars of Light	40
A Story About Pianos	41
The Wonderfully Clear Transition	42

Dina Hardy

Annotated Passengers (Song)	44
Annotated Passengers (Superstition)	50
Annotated Passengers (Sadness)	54
Annotated Passengers (You)	55

Paul Lieber

Hollows	60
Tax Season	61
You Left Your Coat	62
Then It Became a Szechuan Café	63
Almost	64
The First Stripper or Where Is Jeffrey?	66

A Request	67
Nonjudgmental	68
Empty	69
I Don't Want to Turn an Accident into a Poem but when	71
Breeze	72
Slow Return	73

Sarah Maclay

A Breathing Lake	75
A Mirror of Leaves	76
Real State	79
After Vuillard	81
It Is Not a Bridge	83
Rehearsal for Ending	84
Hunger	87
Before Us	88

Holaday Mason

So, What if the Chimes Are Silent?	91
And Both of Us Saw Tiny Spears of Violet	93
Beauty	95
Shrine	96
Fire	97
Menopause	98
Prism	99
The Edge of the World	101
Neptune Chorale	102
Highway 99	104
Towards the Forest	105
From the Mountain to the Prairie to the Oceans, White With Foam	106

Jim Natal

Reading Lao Tzu, Sun Mountain, Santa Fe	109
Sweet Home Chicago	110
The Sense of Touch	112
Rain in L.A.	113

Moses 114
Saguaro Motel 116
Tree of Life Hotel 117
Walking the Beach in the 21st Century 118
The Half-Life of Memory 120
Three Fates 121
Blur 124

Jan Wesley

Day One 126
That Lingering Need for Ritual 128
Taking Cover 129
Nothing Tied Down 131
Great Escapes 132
Inner Ear 133
Elegy Two: Knowing 134
Rough Trade 136
Lying on the Floor and Lying to Oneself Are Equal in Stature ... 137
Come On and Take It 138
History Repeats Itself, Repeats Itself 140
Bleed 142
Love Fallen to the Ground 143

Brenda Yates

Alphabet-flower ABC's 145
Brevity 146
Dream Song Philtre 147
Cauldron of Blue Light 148
Even Without the Minotaur, ... 152
"Death is Nothing" 153
Safe 154
Go in Abstraction by Sevens with Adverbs 155
Seventeen Syllables Searching for Branches 157
Interlude: Kyoto 158
Nightmares 159

Mariano Zaro

After the Diagnosis	161
Enzymes	163
Vocative	165
The Weight of Sound	167
On a Silver Platter	168
At the Studio	170
Brother	171
Mouth to Mouth	173

Acknowledgments 176

Preface
The Venice Collective

The miraculous relationships among the poets in this anthology started more than two decades ago in the public workshops at Midnight Special bookstore in Santa Monica and Beyond Baroque Literary Arts Center in Venice. I, for one, can still recall many of the poems read by the participants then. Those words and images linger and resonate, as does the constructive feedback that has helped our work evolve.

After meeting in those original workshops, we continued to gather, read our work aloud to one another, and offer comments and suggestions. With divergent styles, we've developed and improved our craft yet have managed to retain our distinct voices and mutual respect. Over the years we've become close friends with whom we share our deepest selves by means of our individual poetic ventures—writing, publishing, teaching, reading, and hosting. This has been an unanticipated and undeniable odyssey for us all.

—Paul Lieber

Marjorie Becker

Marjorie Becker is the author of six books, including the critical studies *Dancing on the Sun Stone: Mexican Women and the Gendered Politics of Octavio Paz* (University of New Mexico, 2022) and *Setting the Virgin on Fire: Lázaro Cárdenas, Michoacán Peasants and the Redemption of the Mexican Revolution* (University of California Press, 1995), and three poetry collections, most recently, *The Macon Sex School: Songs of Tenderness and Resistance* (Tebot Bach, 2020), whose first run quickly sold out.

    A Pushcart Prize nominee, she has received an array of awards including a Faculty Fulbright Research Fellowship for Mexico, a USC Mellon Mentoring Award, and awards from the NEH, AAUW, and ACLU. A Macon, Georgia Jewish native, she is multi-lingual and served in the Peace Corps in rural Paraguay. She holds a Yale doctorate and is Professor of History and English at the University of Southern California. She lives in Santa Monica.

The Inner Utter Other Ways to Stay, to Splay, to Rearrange the Silk and its Eternities in Satin and Survival Lust When Dozing There and Then Recall the Sense of Scenery, the Nonchalance Required to Cook, There and Then to Sense How Women Made it, Make it Still within the World of Happenstance and Brilliant Strokes upon the Riled-up Piano Keys of Being

At the guard rail, protecting bolts of sudden silk,
and there Shareina and her nightfall cousin sat beside the densest

satin, lingering close enough within the grace of time and patience when
Marissa Kay and Clara Holm both reappeared

as though those sisters knew just how and who
to see, to feel, to make believe

the time the cottage and the courage
felt such disrepair yet ha!

And ha again, the women knew
just how to scent the scenery,

to sky the shy emotive scenes which
Benjamin, Arnulfo too, they saw and

said, reminding all the others how the
sex itself, it told them when to make their leaps,

to sing, to bring the hot gardenias,
allowing them to soothe and shiver

new beginnings. Did I say that
Benjamin, so plaintive, still remembered how

and when to follow women's leads
and also how to curry favors

from the shy Shareina by—and that
brighter sun, Shasheila—by the

guard rail, now undone, unsung,
and unrepentant as the women there,

they each depend upon the keenest kindest
inner realms of wherewithal and raw

allure and each begins, just hear it now, revere
them now, their fingers fondle, clasp, display

the wildest wanton wayward sounds, they learned
and yearned to move their hands against mahogany,

its color and its numbers, and to wander into
sound itself, surrounding men and boys as well

with sudden burst, a keen repast, the ways and splays
of elegance, the time, those realms they thundered

and decided to return the favors, strip the voices, gather up and
share cantata, open fugue and recipes.

Shad, Malomars

As a child, I sensed that *things*—
exquisite and such costly objects—

matter most to Mama, to our German-Jewish
relatives. The items that defined their thoughts, their words,

their gestures, too, were silver, linens sporting monograms,
as though such articles could laugh and share the night.

Or perhaps the shad in spring, asparagus
provided them with something more than nourishment.

It seemed they so believed in objects' value,
did not consider hugs, the inner lives

of sheer embrace, concern for us
as children, no, not there, no, none of that.

Yet also for the child I was
the nights at Grandma Ida's,

Daddy's Russian Jewish people and thus
my people too, conspired. My Grandma and her youngest

sister Lillie smiled and hugged us in. They fed us treats,
the store-bought cookie-cakes,

those Malomars of happiness;
Aunt Lillie sat upon the floor with us for

Candy Land, some card games too,
and on those evenings Grandma at her

piano prompted dreams and schemes.
of dance, a somehow sudden gracious untold chance.

Encased, Ablaze with Gold

Delray arrived to say the cruelest people meant
to harm, but pay no mind, he said

before he also said *I love your calmest care,*
the ways you recollect

the oldest dreams, repair, the fact
intact you strip the dream, the inner

beams of light and longing, how
the hungry child arrives, abides for you

to feel, undo the pain, retain your grace,
and there and then erase.

You own a hallowed hut, a one-chance home,
a key to dream the schemes of light and I,

Delray, they say I walk your ground,
your soul, your sound, encased,

replaced, engaged, amazed by
light and yes, its wildest ways,

its longing for a heat, a hope
ablaze.

The Stash of Jewels Hiding Far Away Within the Purple Dense, the True Intense, So Come Around, the Ground Revives the Pawn Shop Near the River's Sight, its Succulence

Peter Kahn returned to me, he'd found
a broken amethyst, oh, he a shy

serene magician who had learned
the linings of my underworld, where

just a sigh—the scenery of sighs and sights—
provided blues; the amethyst retained the

story of that long ago, that night when
Peter knew, renewed his dense desire for such

a moment, then another near the emeralds
and the rubies I had deeper, darker wild

retrained from energies of sigh so close to
moments as momentous when we women

at the Purple Pawn decided there and then
to give away our themes for song, for

symphonies we somehow saw and then
began to wear the trove of gemstones

and whenever Peter stripped
away pretense, reminding me he'd

brought me back the sapphire lights I made,
the somehow night together we had

long ago chanced, we'd danced within that dawn,
oh melody . . .

Voices from the Macon Purple Pawn
In memory of Elsa Kessler and Marjorie Ruth Kahn Popper

What was missing in that daunted
world mistreating Blacks as though
by rule and Jews like us unseen, unheard,

yes, what was missing there in Georgia
was a music in the wild, unclaimed,
an instrumental female flame, a fire

that warmed a need to share, reveal
a widespread heat, a gentle chance
to learn, discern, return to

language filled with sustenance,
with flavors ripe as spice,
such flavors full of deep insight

like Cousin Elsa's mocha roll, as she,
her husband Max, the refugees my
grandma's funds recovered, yes,

her food, her sense that sweets like
mocha roll existed there in Macon, where
these fantasies might there, might then,

might now begin to sing, to bring an unheard light
by night, by noon when notes themselves emerged without,
within, becoming there and then a somehow

symphony we there, we then, began to sense beyond,
within again, again, to bring.

When Diamonds Found the Ways Without, Within

She knew the nest of diamonds revealed
its light, the wild collected shapes, the oblongs and the
central circles spoke, retained a deep display of chatter,
scatter, keen aplomb upon a wrist as open-handed, tactile

as my grandma's since she also played and taught piano in that
midst of time; she knew the nest, the best of gemstones there in Macon
proved that she, my Grandma Ida could bestow the light, the wilderness
of colors coming on past dawn and at the total tonal teas a group, oh

such a bunch of sumptuous socialites arriving there from foreign towns
once filled with Jews, revealing all the workings and the wonder of
the figs, the grapes, the ways to sense, repent of cruelties in
Macon's wished-for harbor near some water and some remedies.

When Ida played piano there and then she took her heavy, heartfelt
bracelet off; her breath, its breadth just loaded down with luster
born so far away and resting there in Macon just to shimmer, never
simmer in the heat of song . . .

Replete with Seers Singing Scheme, the Sapphire Light Itself Prepared a Theme, a Way to Wonder, Blunder, Ponder Flight as Generous as Porch Light When It Comes Around, Illuminates the Skies of Peace and Wild Prosperities Again, Again, Again, and Once Again

My cousin Trix and I possessed the Purple Unknown
Pawn, a store where we continued there
to strip to inner notions of the dreams we read, the schemes we bred,
the wilderness of cruelties we trained the broken men, the women
full of fears like mine to flee; we owned a song, a throng replenished all
the sapphires we had claimed each time we simply sighed and
beckoned, reckoned depth within the pawn we gave away the
extra fried and okra we prepared to share, repair, maintain as we were
chefs as well as Jewish merchants there in Macon in the morning.

The Wingéd Wild Abides, Abides, Bestows, Endures Inside Predictions Spelling Out a Sense of Peace, a Way, a Splay, a Place Where Here We Sense We See, We Wing the Newest Naked Notion Placed Where Peace Itself Might Murmur, Shimmer, Settle

The panic of deep desire,
the knowledge only here,

this might-fall panic purple
only only stops because we say the word,

the cries unheard when those who still controlled broke,
undid the world. I mentioned that,

then turned because my mention meant a sudden set,
the wings the goddess of the depth bestowed,

this poem about an energy,
the poem about a reason that I flew to Mexico,

yes, this poem a search about the search I once
decided might provide me custodies of art,

of light, of longing for this wingéd fire,
a piece of wingéd peace and flan from

far away or deep within the songs,
the throng of light

that somehow still arrives,
abides within.

What We Didn't Do and What We Did

Those early mornings, up and on the brick-house
porch so very close and sheltered by

an aging oak, its acorns as quiet
as we: just waiting, Daddy, me,

the heat-to-be so dense, intense yet
later on, as we were waiting there so calm,

expectant, and it's true I never cried with Daddy,
never felt untended, no, we also didn't

make the food for breakfast as Mama would,
nor sweep the porch nor even,

rake the leaves that later showered down.
We also didn't celebrate nor conjugate

our happiness together there,
but rather waited for the paperboy,

whose name was Walter Bryant,
when he rode his bike toward us

tossing us a smile, another,
a copy of *The Macon Telegraph*.

Pie Filling

At dawn and in the Purple Unspent Pawn,
we made a harbor pie,

the food we felt we'd eat,
would share in wildly unlit circumstance

if only men began to sense, to see
the female wonder,

worlds beyond the tonal plunder men like one-time Jeff
revealed and then,

because he sensed my hope and care,
we women learned again right then, right there

a way to stand our ground, awaiting
ripest berries from the backyard wild

that we believed could feed and feel
the need, oh yes, the true concern for dance

right then and later too when we maintain
within my store out back a sort of true

imbued provision we decided we should give,
acclaim, retain, because our flavored open colors,

true refrain emerged
as sudden remedy.

Golden Feather Once Forlorn, Unborn, Adrift, Arrives Decides How Fate Can, There within the Purple Pawn Shop, Ponder Light, Abide

What is there, Shareina asked, to trade.
The men arrived still disarranged

and someone in the back believes
they stole my topaz from my

dense and unrepentant grandmama who plied
such notions, nether notes and then again

I like the thought of chords' reply,
the ways the colors slither when relieved

so where are we and why, I ask,
so purple. Why a chandelier aloft,

what kind of breeze becomes a lady
and a topaz. Do we think enough

within the lives of gems whose beings
brighten sense, repentance yet again.

My pawn shop lives because the men
reply by nights that bring about

a golden feathered dawn, the
feathers wild, retired, aspiring

wings, the wind itself a hint to just
engage a way to splay the stay

a while and frolic in this store
where I adore the men

arrive and then again begin to farm
the food out back, the wingéd feast,

the slipper peas and okra.

Restoration of Macon's Temple after the 2023 Fascist Attack

Are there songs, he asked,
he touched me. Then, a true massage

of care, repair, the listened, yes
to hear, revere, the songs around me

as I wandered in, began again.
I owned a wild and purple store

in which a music could restore
a song of peace, a naked wild

attempt to feed *at need*, to feel
within, again, again and listen to

the topaz, yes, the amethyst, the
quartz itself all glisten in a

chorus, in a profound way of
splaying peace and ripe

display of early morning fruit and
schemes, an open theme of care,

repair.

They Bought My Time So Cheaply

I thought I might, it was polite, to give, and give, yes give away
again the only time I knew I had a moment, only that, no more,

no less, so why this constant courtesy, this waste of just a moment,
only that, no more, when "no" itself a word unheard in times like this

where Jewish Southern women trained toward "yes," though "yes"
remembers now and how that "no" itself a deep response, a destiny

where peace just breathes, it saunters, then surrenders toward
a sudden sheer, and hear it now, revere it too, it was, it is

so silken and melodious.

Summer Fruit

Seeking sudden solace, I re-described
his hidden name when he arrived
as though to beckon, beg for wild
and only summer fruit,

a melon I prepared, some cheese that
I believed he loved, though then again
we often fed each other, waiting,
then displaying reconnection and
eternities of touch itself,

premonition.

How We Orchestrated Macon in the Wild

How to enter song, the throng
of notes' deliverance and how

to know their musings, inner care
that music then, that music there

provided in our nights of pause,
reprieve, we *made* those worlds,

we singers did, in high relief,
in utter calm, we knew through breath

a way, refrain of sheer intense belief
and hot and wild concern

we surely burned by night and its proclaim.

Jeanette Clough

Jeanette Clough holds an M.A from the University of Chicago, Division of the Humanities, and worked as an art librarian at the Getty Research Institute in Los Angeles. Her book *Flourish* was a finalist in the Otis College of Art and Design and Eastern Washington University book competitions. Other publications include *Island*, from Red Hen, as well as two artist books, *Stone* and *Rx*, from Conflux. A poetry collection is forthcoming from Cahuenga Press.

Her poetry received awards in the Los Angeles Poetry Festival Fin de Millennium, Ruskin Art Club, and Rainer Maria Rilke International Poetry competitions, and a Commendation in the *Aesthetica* Creative Works competition (UK). She was an artist-in-residence for the National Parks/Joshua Tree where she taught writing workshops for many years. Among the journals publishing her poems are *Atlanta Review, Colorado Review, Denver Quarterly,* and the *Laurel Review*. Clough served as a poetry editor for *Solo, A Journal of Poetry*, and *Foreshock, An Anthology of Poems from the Midnight Special*, and reviewed for *Poetry International*.

Unknown

The unknown sounds like bones rubbing against water.

When you touch the unknown, it almost always retreats.
That's how it remains unknown.

The unknown looks like the inner rim of an intact eggshell.

It understands nothing of timetables, everything about
hallucinations.

If you try to surprise the unknown, it will give you strange dreams.

Its best colors are carbazole, quinacridone, and phthalo.

When the unknown takes a break, it makes the same sound
as a paisley couch.

It understands everything about mysticism, nothing of blueprints.

Occasionally blueprints show a door in the wrong place.
This is the unknown telling a joke.

Occasionally someone thinks they can explain the unknown,
which also makes the unknown laugh.

From this we learn the unknown has a sense of humor.

When the unknown laughs, it makes a sound like waves receding
over gravel. Stand in the surf and find out.

The laughter of the unknown is contagious and may wash you
out to sea.

Antonym: photogenic. Synonym: flicker.

The unknown never does the same thing twice.

Then again, maybe it does. Who knows?

The unknown stores its names in the rings of Saturn, and downloads them into the rings of trees.

When you hear something round, that's the unknown saying its name, over and over.

Imagining the Desert Trumpet

It could be the desert trumpet plant tastes like talc,
or how I imagine talc would taste since I have tasted

neither. If I did (for this is the work of imagination)
both would be chalky. Because I have not seen

the desert trumpet, I can say it will look like kelp
dried stiff, beached forever a long way from water,

and slightly amber. The smell is a newly discovered
place not yet named, so I imagine the place and its name,

and that their scent is like the desert trumpet. The feel
is the hard wings of a beetle I have never touched,

or like a remembered shell. The bloom is quiet. Or rather,
it makes the sound before Joshua trumpeted, I imagine.

Silver Reef

I park my car under the translucent leaves. On the right,
two motorcycles.

Everything has a crust. The crust sparkles. Salt, thorns,
a semi-precious sheen.

I am off the map again, among the crystal trees.

The Interstate says Silver Reef, and I veer like ore to the magnet.

The sky is lavender and the rocks are Martian red.
A pack of tumbleweeds does not touch the ground.

My eyes are fooling me. The order in which things may have happened:

>   Dogs across from my motel do not recognize me.
>   I forget to watch the sunset.
>   Tire rims litter the highway with their rubber cuticle.
>   I expect another scenic off-road vista.

Thukk of insects on the windshield.
A sonic boom splits the heat.

Sandstone in silver, silver in red.
Prospectors did not come here for the view.

Mining cars stenciled *Turquoise* and *Gold* balance
on narrow-gauge rails. The walk-in safe, intact.

Two dry drinking fountains. The caretaker talks to herself
and offers tap water.

She likes to watch people put things together from the displays.
I fall for the rocks and sky.

I could sit in this breeze and drink free water night and day.

The town stares.
I drive its one cul-de-sac road.
I disturb the lizard edge,
the small claws in the underbrush.

A stranger hides his face behind the wheel.
Three men wave hello and drive off on two motorbikes.

Insects in the Desert

Two empty five-gallon jugs.
A decoy water dish kept outside
for the bees that swarm my wet laundry,

clinging like chainmail front to back,
buzzing, drinking the fabric dry.
I pick flies from the kitchen sink

after washing my hair. Power surges,
frequent and theatrical, disrupt the tiny moths.
Later I walk among the ghost trees, fable-like,

densely shadowed, disorienting at first,
no illumination except a sky flocked with stars
until, wingless and homing, I too am drawn

to the sulfur-yellow bulb over the veranda,
the half-full glass sweating on my nightstand.

Moth

The morning routine, soap that dries on its way to your body, then cleaning up the insects that line the lamp's inner rim and whatever gave light or moisture, like the bedside scented oil coated with winged spots, the sinks, tub, and adjacent surfaces—though there's a sharp decrease over the past two days so perhaps this has been their season and they are fluttering toward the next stage of mothness, making more of themselves, transient as torn lettuce, as an ant's ginger mound on a dirt road, lingering, as one left suddenly alone, as drops of oil isolated on a tile floor and never absorbed. Sidestep, just for a moment, winding sideways in loping S's, the early breeze embryonic, soft as a cat's ear brushing your cheek with a hint of cucumber, disentangling, strewing the powdered veil under which you have lived.

The Jasmine Corridor
after J.D.

I know how to enter the storyline from a stale velvet seat screwed into a sticky floor. The screen (its color and smell, its opal shimmer) promises a story meant for me. A Byzantine lure of bells, and your body displays itself in controlled light. My body is a lonely creature. Soon it may commit another crime. I am telling you my secrets. They are small, shameful, and repetitive, the grenadine in a cheap sweet drink. I don't resist the city's floral odors this time of year, especially in the corridor of jasmine. The morning is gray and predictable, the iodine sunset, full of sleep. I wake up in the same bed. Cat, then coffee. I am losing sight of the form, which has to do with the sound prey makes when a lion takes it down by the throat. In the heaven of animals, a gazelle falls in the chase, maimed, dying, and after the lion has eaten its fill, pulls together skin and bone, eye and nose, rising on spindly legs to sniff the air and chance again the open plain.

Heist

As if from the corner of the boxer's ring

I want to know what matters to you
because the same thing matters to me.

The lines that float across your face,
for instance. Your private plans for shelter.

Favorite textures and shirts. I want to know them—
the kind of softness you prefer

against your skin. Not smooth,
but with a nap whose weft rests there easily.

I am not smooth. Consider, we are
matched strands of twine tied into a knot.

Which of your ridges shall I caress first?
Which shall I save until last?

You must tell me, while I thieve your body.

Evocation (Streets)

I am surrounded by streets
that are half-lit, sheathed
by metal and glass, and marbled
with neon-veined red.

The city's body is full of miracles
and sad majesty, drunk
from 24-hour light, so much,
cast onto familiar sidewalks

where I, among the arcades,
the eloquent columns
grown from asphalt,
among the sirens, am lost.

Ardor

                       Take a direction left or right
to the street where oblivious to traffic ballet boys
and ballet girls parade down the center line

swaying on bright muscled legs, roughing up their toes,
brushing the asphalt with lamb's wool and sequins,
with lost elastic and satin ribbons, performing their steps

with a sharp hunger that will solve every problem, with
ardor hard as a rose-cut diamond set in platinum, in angles
that refract and will not, no matter what, be still.

Incognito

A cab, parked at the curb. Driver nowhere
to be seen, like the spokes inside an uncut
lemon, like absence neutral as the beige ruin

of a suburban tract house. Interconnected malls
occupy multiple city blocks, four levels above and
two below. I want to find the Joie de Vivre Motel

where every night the contents of cabinets
rearrange, where 180 Darwinian finches trill
the same cadence at different speeds, where

doors fly open like uncorked champagne,
tilt like orange and azure bird of paradise beaks,
where we live incognito, abundantly, & at home.

Pillars of Light

Everyone sees pillars of light at dusk.

A man descends a luminous shaft like a charm in a floaty pen
and hovers in the lane to her right.

She has heard about these winged men and women
who wear long dresses and are adorned with feathers

so we will understand they have come a long way and will
leave again like migrating geese.

She invites him into her car.

It feels good to drive with the convertible down and a couple of
milky wings streaming over the back fender.

It's L.A. at rush hour, and the beyond baroque twilight settles its
differences with the smog, turning the horizon cinnabar

strewn with construction cranes that rest in their one-leg-resting position
while day goes down and the night shift rises on

platforms to the top floors where men with hammers and blowtorches
work through the dark hours into dawn.

A Story About Pianos

A sea of asphalt is marked with 88 parking spaces. In each space is a player piano. The pianos start automatically but never together or with the same music. They play morning and night, rain or shine. No one can stop the pianos or park their cars. A fleet of bulldozers pushes the pianos together and drives over them until they stop playing. The pianos go elsewhere.

The pianos string their seven octaves 88 times across a field. Each speck of the field has a sound to play. Samba, hip-hop, jitterbug, waltzes, quadrilles, hula, clogging, and krumping composed from downpours, staccato hail, arpeggios of thunder, and the silence of lightning. The lovelorn sigh of ladybugs, a *basso profundo* chorus of roots, crickets' fluty trill, the squeak of sprouting seeds, moth dust, broken quail eggs, a ring of standing stones, loose feathers, tufts of fur, all of it played together dawn through dawn. The field is ploughed under, sold in sod chunks, or mowed, and soon can make almost no sound at all. The pianos go elsewhere.

In the open sea, the pianos continually change direction. The upright player pianos crest a swell. Their piano wire splits into currents, and the keys become foam. A dozen baby grands smash against a massive rock and the harps inside enter the throat of the sea. The sea breaks and heals, then breaks again. The pianos play constantly. Nothing stops them.

The Wonderfully Clear Transition

First, from behind the cypress tree
a block-and-a-half guess away,
its bottle-green scrim filtering
the diminishing hour, its heat,

and she, opening all the drapes
and windows, systematically, from west
to south, east to north, widdershins,
counters the usual arc and instead

tunes to the sudden harmonica player
bending riffs longer than the alley over which
she lives. There are so many gradations
of time and light. Let me explain.

Dina Hardy

Dina Hardy has received a Pratt Institute BFA; Iowa Writers' Workshop MFA; a Stanford Stegner Fellowship; Pushcart nominations; fellowships to residencies in the countries of Georgia, Spain, and Wales; and has been published in journals such as *AQR*, *Bennington Review*, *Black Warrior Review*, *Gulf Coast*, and *Third Coast*.

Annotated Passengers (Song)

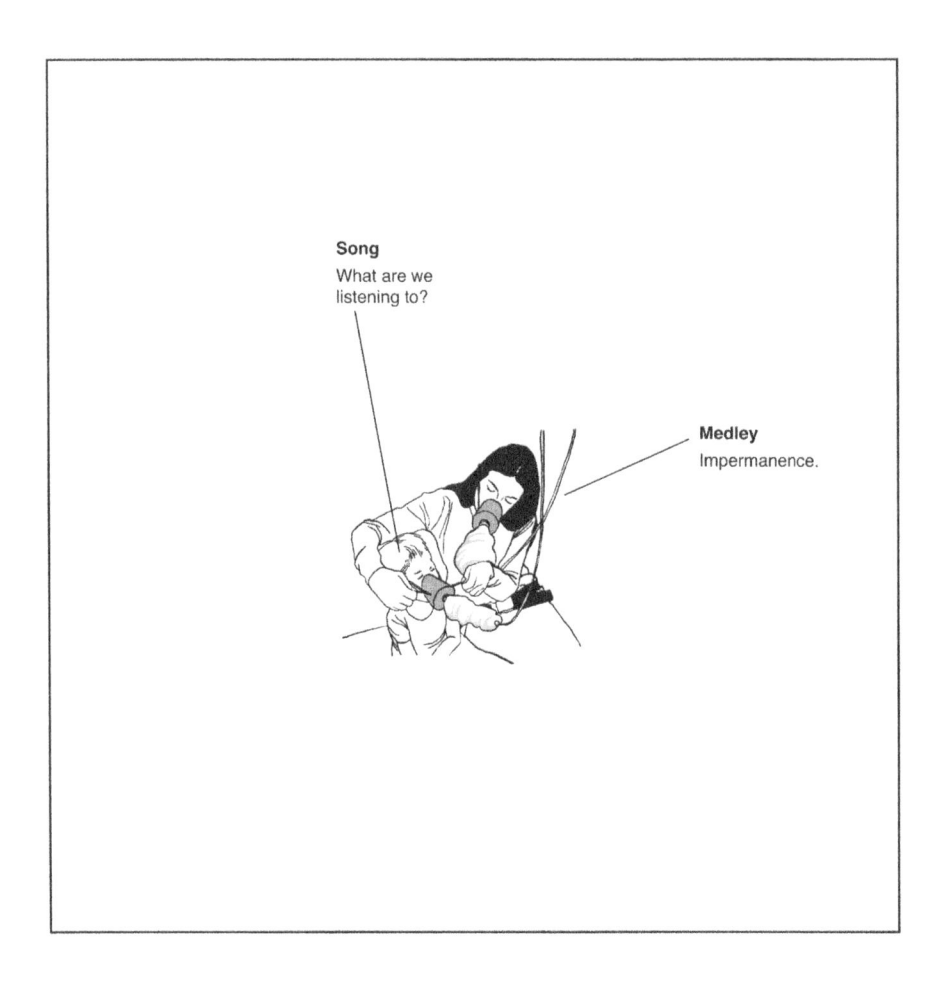

Brun
Here I am
sharing my
soul to you.

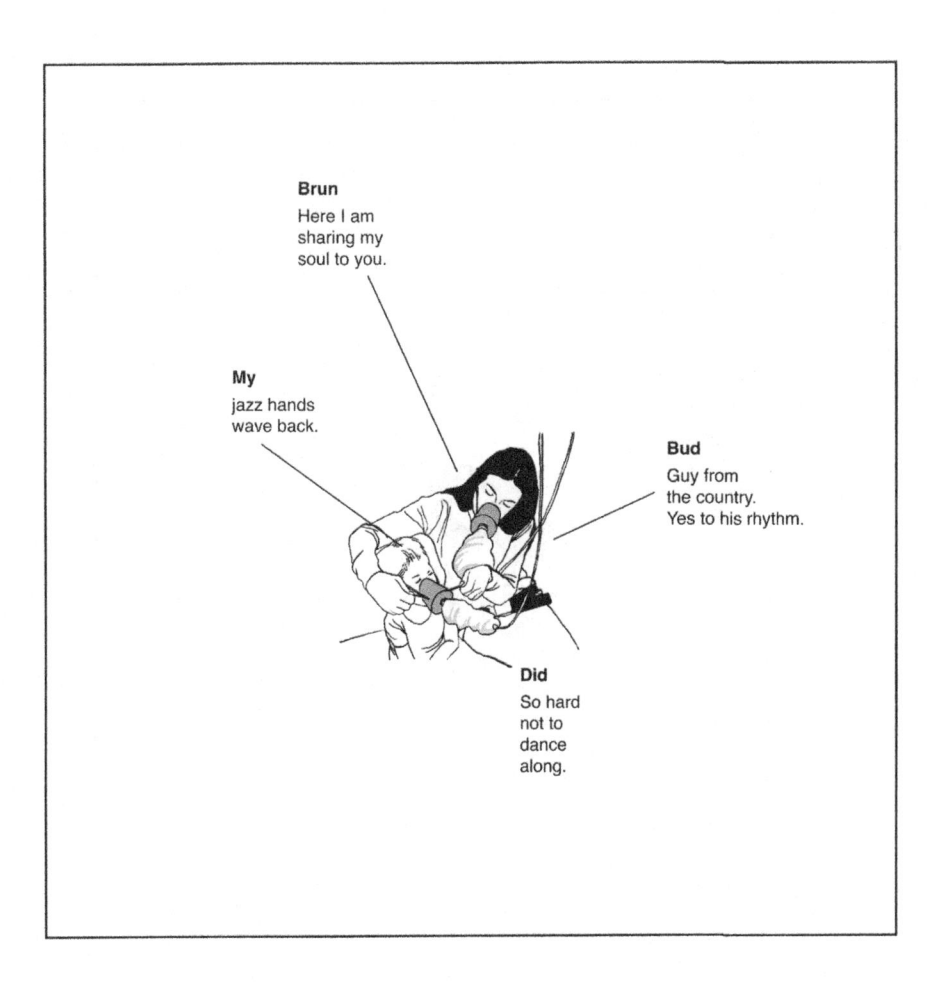

My
jazz hands
wave back.

Bud
Guy from
the country.
Yes to his rhythm.

Did
So hard
not to
dance
along.

Dina Hardy 45

Baby
I'll do backup
vocals. I can really
do a wo wo.

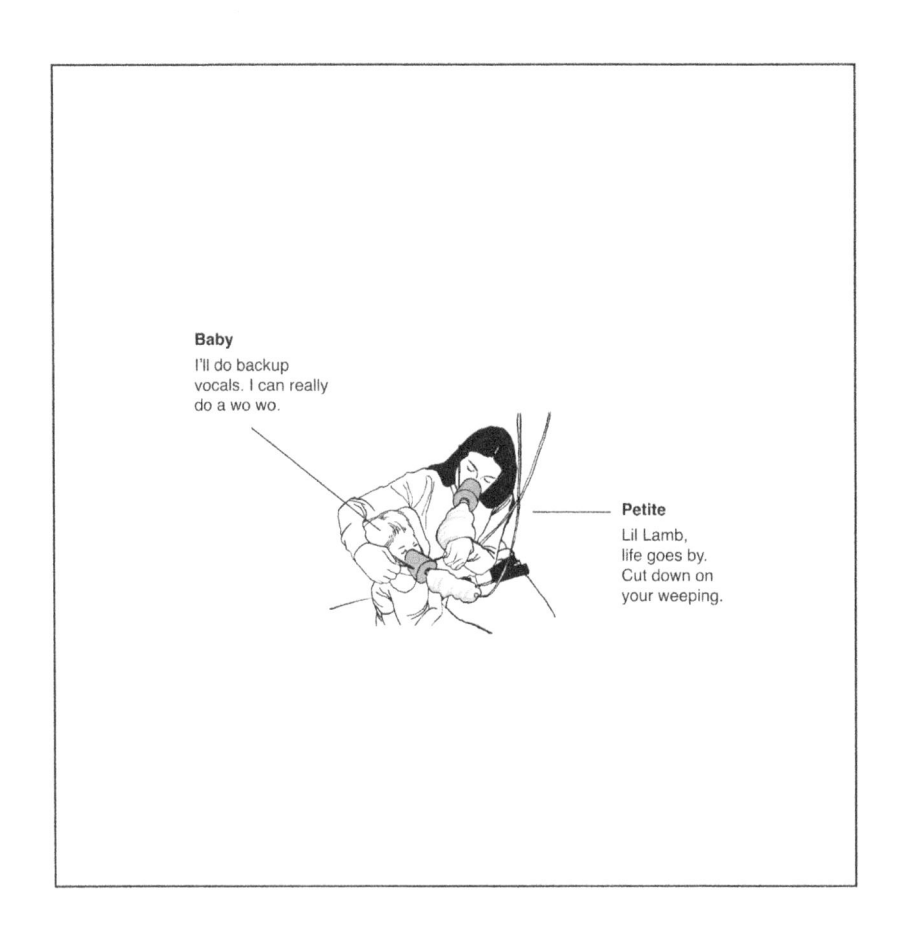

Petite
Lil Lamb,
life goes by.
Cut down on
your weeping.

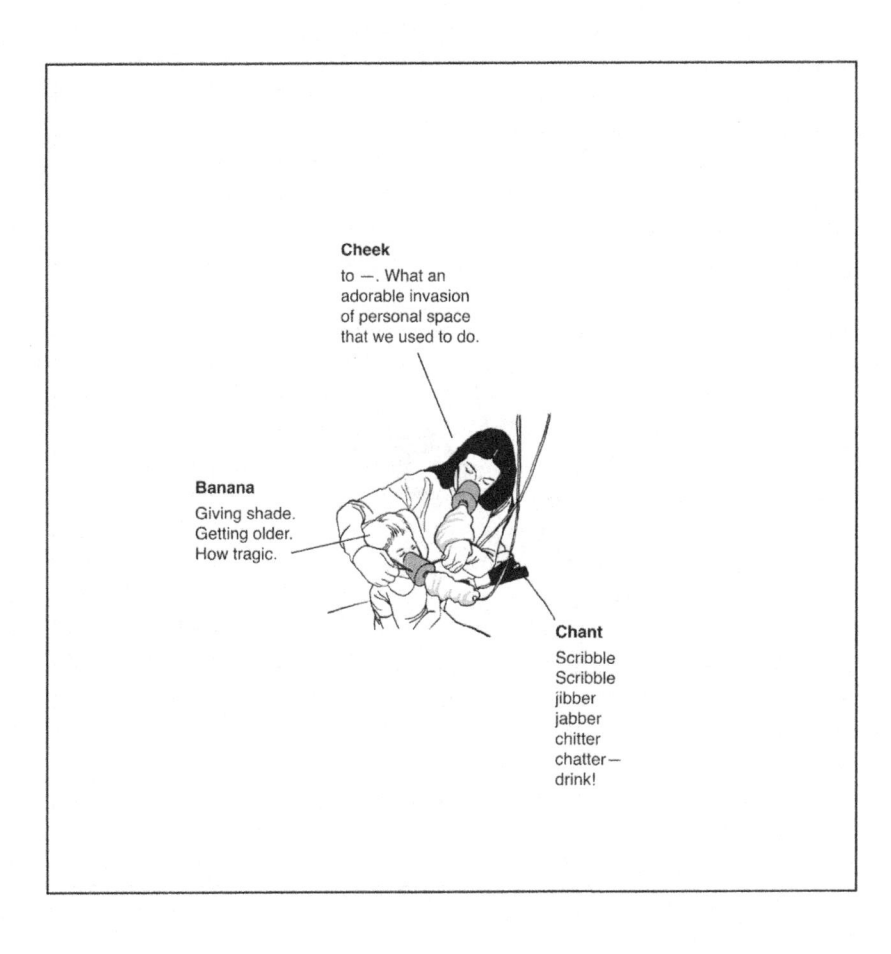

Cheek
to —. What an adorable invasion of personal space that we used to do.

Banana
Giving shade. Getting older. How tragic.

Chant
Scribble
Scribble
jibber
jabber
chitter
chatter—
drink!

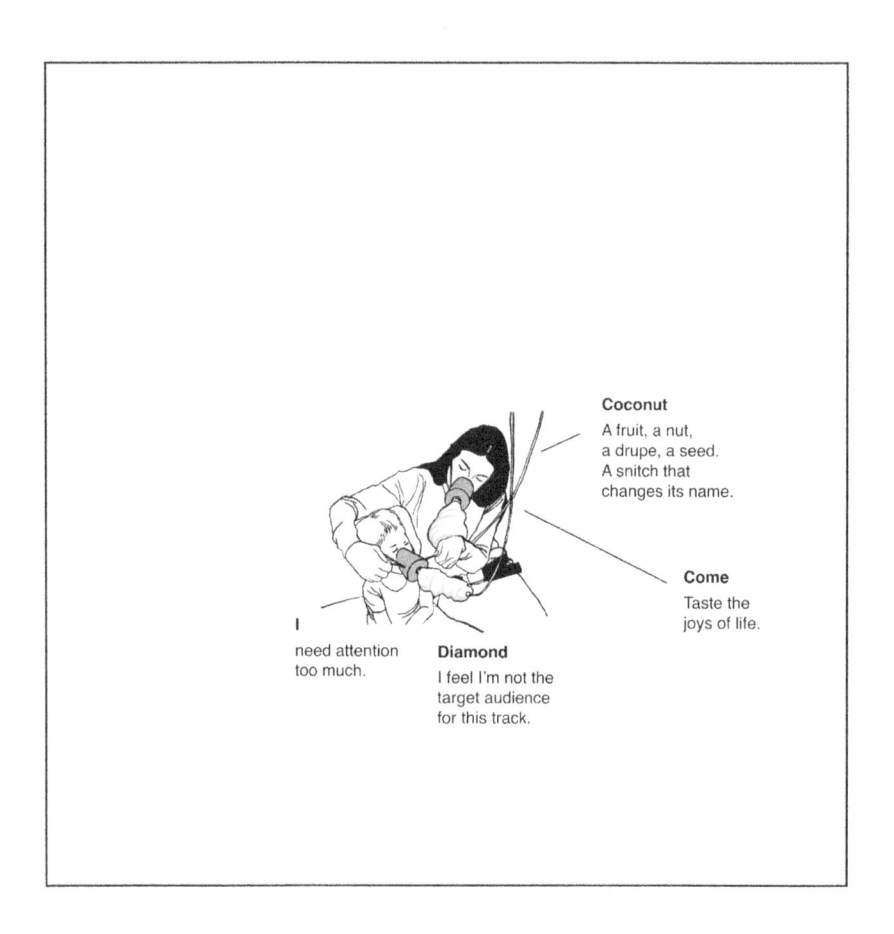

Coconut
A fruit, a nut,
a drupe, a seed.
A snitch that
changes its name.

Come
Taste the
joys of life.

I
need attention
too much.

Diamond
I feel I'm not the
target audience
for this track.

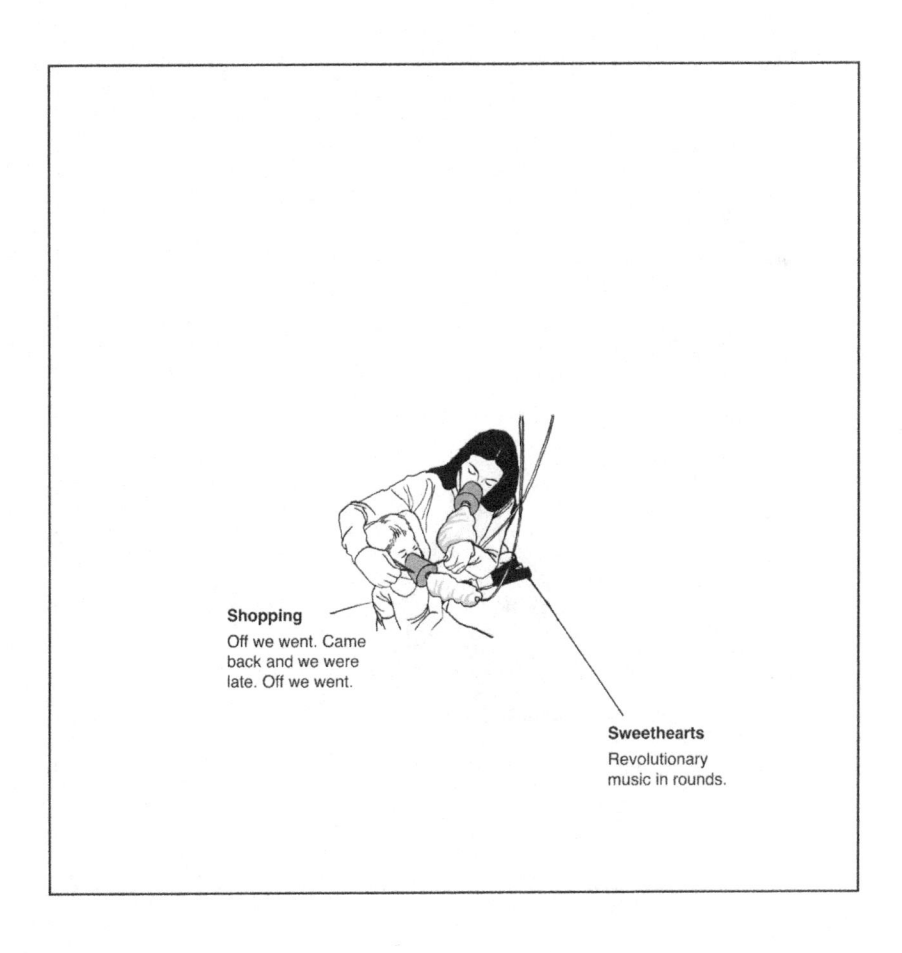

Shopping
Off we went. Came
back and we were
late. Off we went.

Sweethearts
Revolutionary
music in rounds.

Annotated Passengers (Superstition)

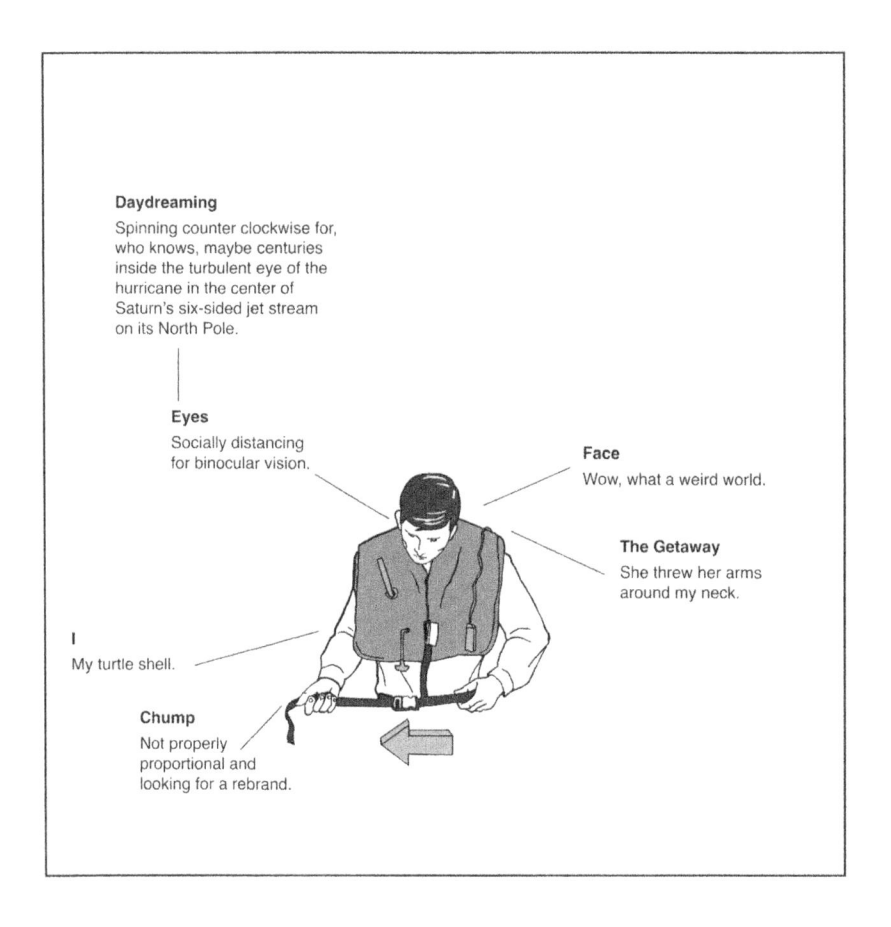

Daydreaming
Spinning counter clockwise for, who knows, maybe centuries inside the turbulent eye of the hurricane in the center of Saturn's six-sided jet stream on its North Pole.

Eyes
Socially distancing for binocular vision.

Face
Wow, what a weird world.

The Getaway
She threw her arms around my neck.

I
My turtle shell.

Chump
Not properly proportional and looking for a rebrand.

Manteca
on a hot griddle, aka walking in the full force of a city summer.

Summer
The sun just sprang from my head. Oh, that's nice and smokey.

Superstition
Sometimes you have a thought and get a little bonus with it.

Change

You've got it bad, girl. /
You've got it, bad girl. /
You've got...(pause).
It...(pause). Bad...(thinking).
Girl...(unfinished thought). /
You got it /
You me, let's get bad, girl.

Love
Flying a little too close to
the sun, either this is all
about me or nothing is;
who's to say.

Love
Flipping to the B side,
either this is all about
you or nothing is;
who's to say.

Dina Hardy

Annotated Passengers (Sadness)

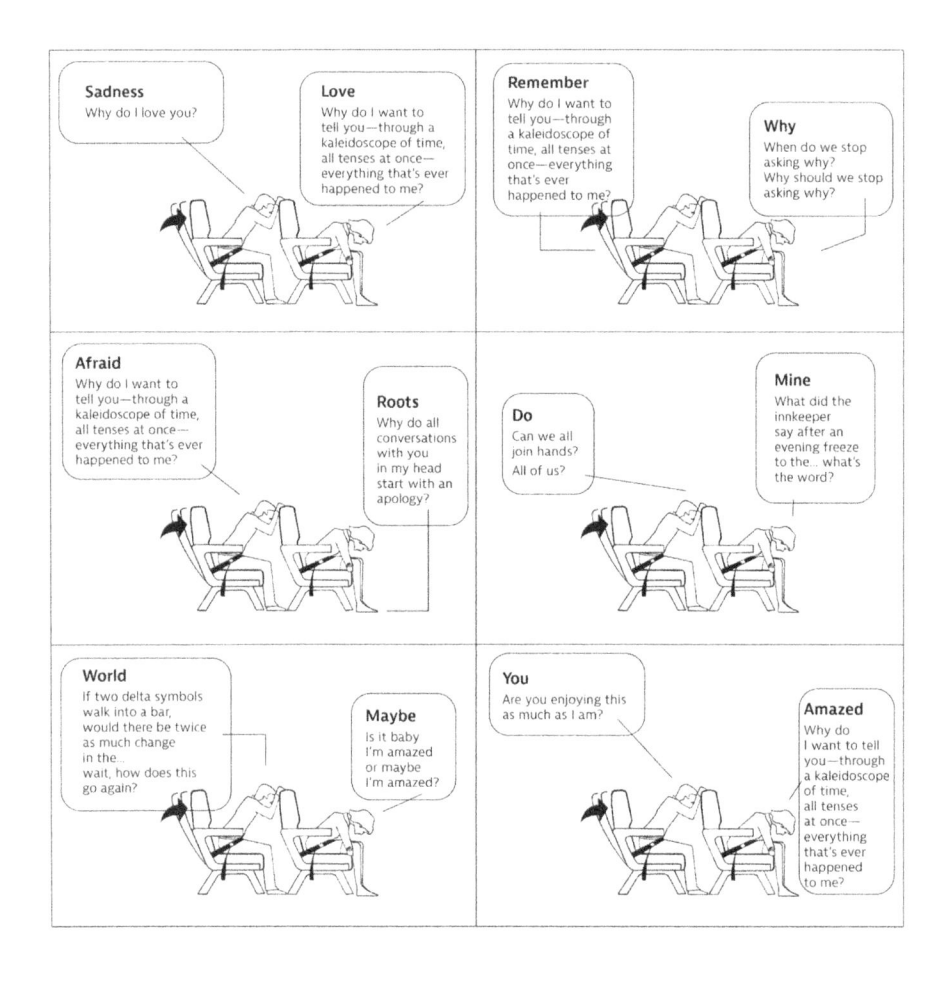

Sadness
Why do I love you?

Love
Why do I want to tell you—through a kaleidoscope of time, all tenses at once—everything that's ever happened to me?

Remember
Why do I want to tell you—through a kaleidoscope of time, all tenses at once—everything that's ever happened to me?

Why
When do we stop asking why? Why should we stop asking why?

Afraid
Why do I want to tell you—through a kaleidoscope of time, all tenses at once—everything that's ever happened to me?

Roots
Why do all conversations with you in my head start with an apology?

Do
Can we all join hands? All of us?

Mine
What did the innkeeper say after an evening freeze to the... what's the word?

World
If two delta symbols walk into a bar, would there be twice as much change in the... wait, how does this go again?

Maybe
Is it baby I'm amazed or maybe I'm amazed?

You
Are you enjoying this as much as I am?

Amazed
Why do I want to tell you—through a kaleidoscope of time, all tenses at once—everything that's ever happened to me?

Annotated Passengers (You)

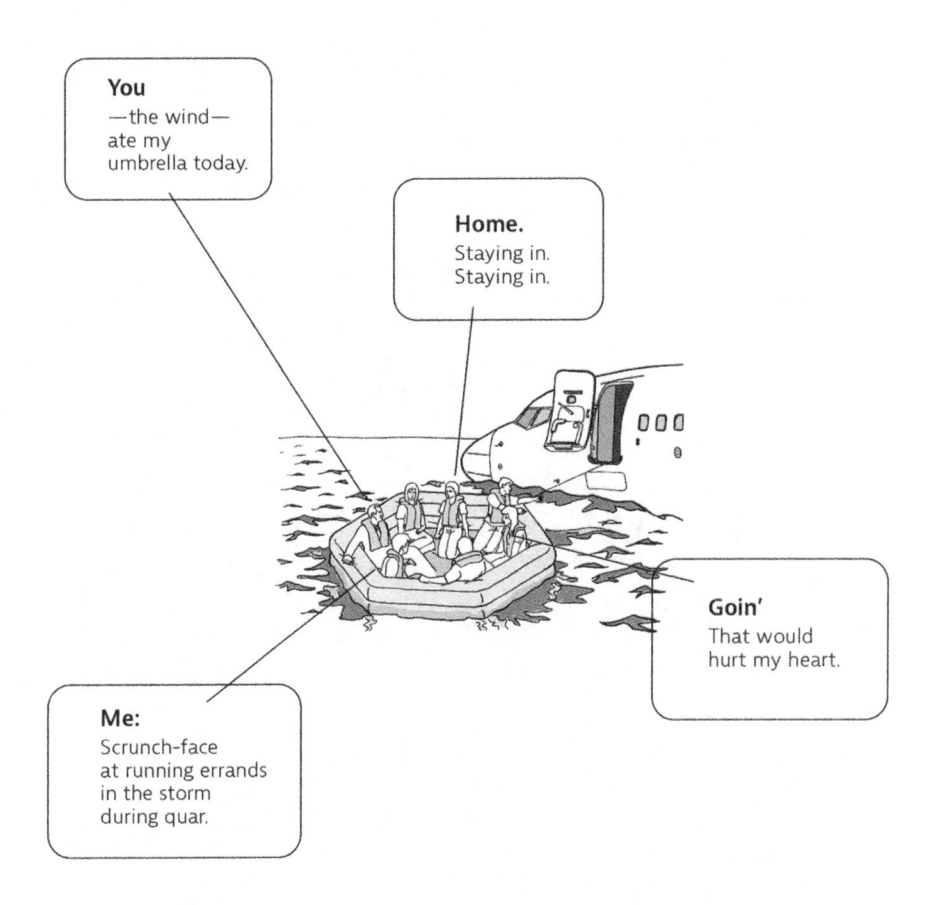

You
—the wind—
ate my
umbrella today.

Home.
Staying in.
Staying in.

Goin'
That would
hurt my heart.

Me:
Scrunch-face
at running errands
in the storm
during quar.

I,
Thor,
mansplaining
the clouds.

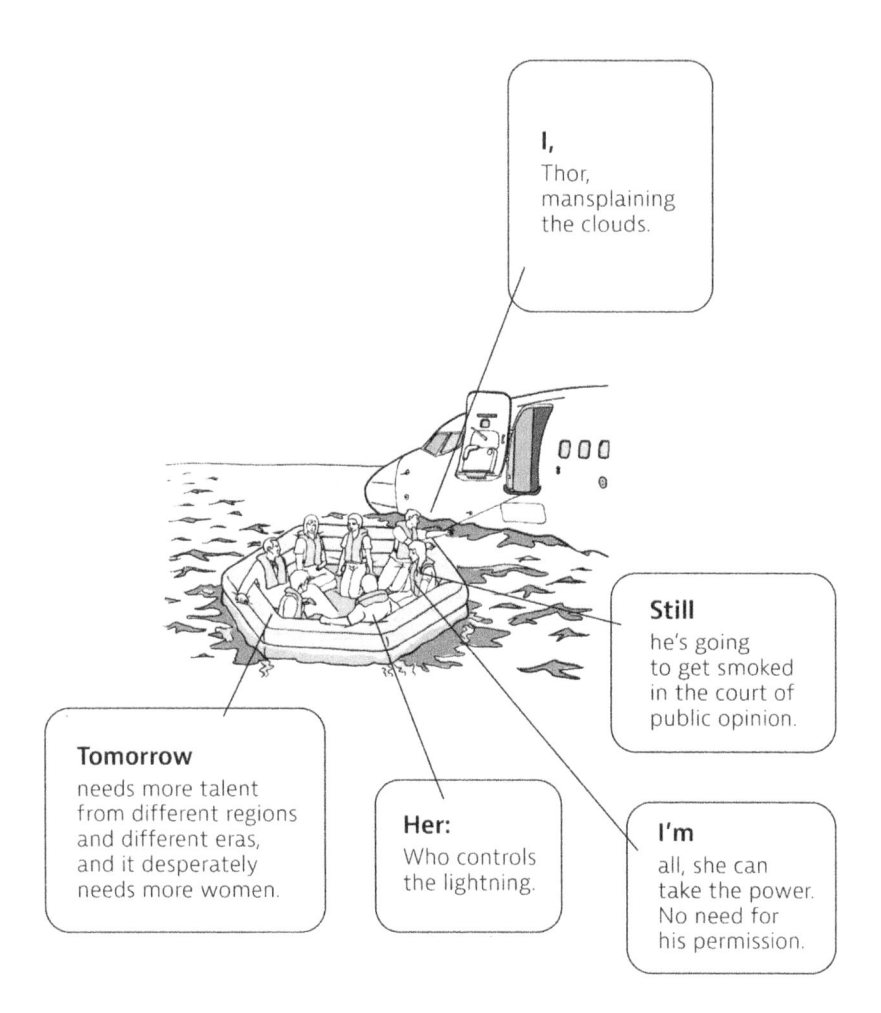

Still
he's going
to get smoked
in the court of
public opinion.

Tomorrow
needs more talent
from different regions
and different eras,
and it desperately
needs more women.

Her:
Who controls
the lightning.

I'm
all, she can
take the power.
No need for
his permission.

'Cause
They're going
to go celebrate
how they're
going to celebrate.

'Cause
Verzez vs
versus vs
Vs vs V v
Who won?

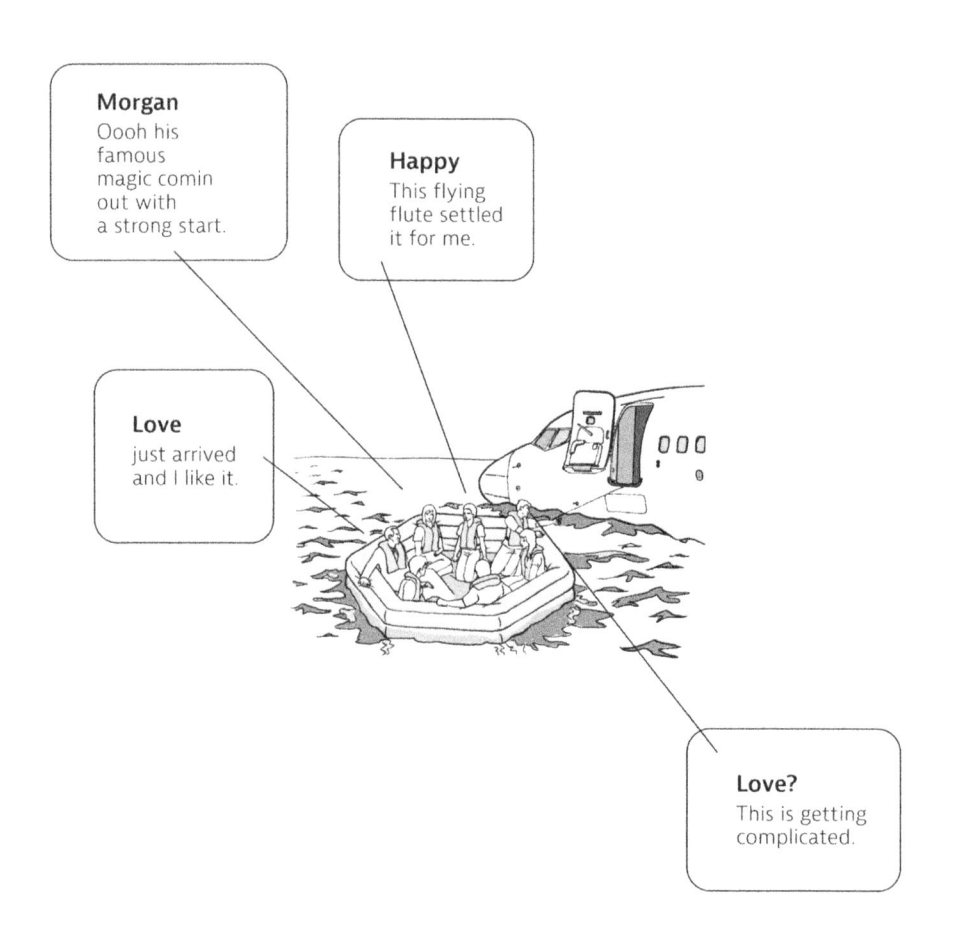

Morgan
Oooh his famous magic comin out with a strong start.

Happy
This flying flute settled it for me.

Love
just arrived and I like it.

Love?
This is getting complicated.

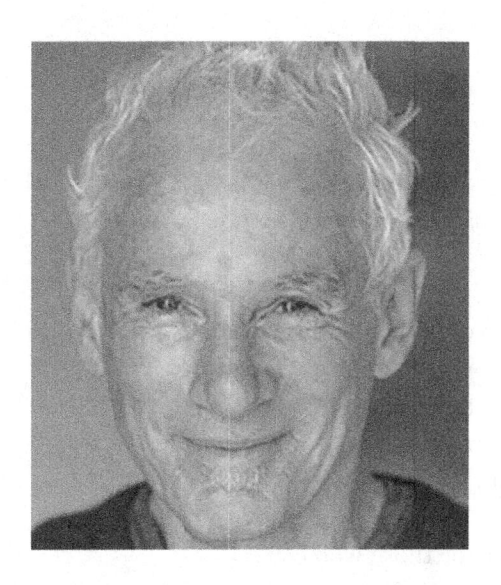

Paul Lieber

Interrupted by the Sea, Paul's second collection of poetry, was published by What Books Press, which will release his third collection, *Slow Return*, in 2024. His first collection, *Chemical Tendencies*, was published by Tebot Bach. He received an honorable mention in the Allen Ginsberg Contest. Three times nominated for a Pushcart Prize, Paul produced and hosted "Why Poetry" on Pacifica radio in LA. Paul's poems have appeared in *The Moth, N.Y. Quarterly, Paterson Literary Review, Askew, Poemeleon, Alimentum*, and many other journals and anthologies. He has taught Poetry at Loyola Marymount University and facilitated the poetry workshop at Beyond Baroque, the oldest literary institute in Los Angeles. Paul works as an actor. He currently teaches acting at AMDA.

Hollows

The Willowbrook day room
for the mentally retarded, Jan. 19, 1972 (photos)

—Fred W. McDarrah, *Anarchy, Protest, and Rebellion:*
And the Counterculture That Changed America (p. 320)

Where the deprived are deprived.
One, naked, sits on a chair with his legs
crossed. Another finds peace
in sleep in the corner.
A boy contorts in a yoga-like
pose. It's the destination
for the forgotten, for those who can't
dress themselves. A girl outside
the frame screams and bites
her knees and wrists. Her name is Cindy.
She has three different voices.
All originate from the stains and grime
that cover the walls; all are ominous.
Now she rocks back and forth
to the lullabies she never heard.
She finds comfort in her sway.
The residents in a lower photo
lie down with a camera above
to shock us into legal action.
The bones of these infants could have been
shipped from Buchenwald.
The pencil-thin legs reveal starvation.
You can see below the skin,
into the hollows. Stop and weep
a few moments and then return.
Return to the boy's face—
who looks like I did as a boy.

Tax Season

My father buried
at the kitchen table
under stacks of papers
fingers a calculator.
He prepares his taxes.
He can't be bothered.
His humor swept away.
Bankrupt,
he perspires.
Is he crying?
Not now but
yes
when he revealed
the time
he walked in
on his mother
turning a trick.
After that she
never looked at him.
After that
she never recognized him.
And after that
she took up residence
in Rockland State Mental Hospital.
But now my father
fights the IRS
deducting and deducting
until no one owes anyone
anything.

You Left Your Coat
In memory of George Murdoch

last night
the tacky hip length one
you'd always wear
but you were not
in my dream so how
did it get there?
George, you called me
before
going into heart surgery
perhaps coincidental
perhaps to say goodbye
but for me it was just a call
our photo together
on the album cover
leans on top
of the bookshelf
perhaps you could enter
my dream in full
some night
perhaps tonight
and reclaim your coat
the dream was not about your coat
just a prop, an incidental
a passing object
or thought
but it was yours George
definitely yours
really nothing to see
just hanging out
with you missing

Then It Became a Szechuan Café

Hasidic men with traditional fur felt hats
at Crown Heights gathering (photo)

—Fred W. McDarrah, *Anarchy, Protest, and Rebellion:*
And the Counterculture That Changed America (p. 75)

There's a line of Hasidic men with fur-felt hats
with no date at the bottom of the photo;
they've remained in the same garb
for centuries, the same unbending
beliefs and the mystery encased
in the Torah—the mystery
of the mystery in the mystery.
They could argue among themselves
and God, hats in place and payos growing.
I might as well be Christian, Muslim,
Buddhist, an atheist among them,
an infidel who gobbles Gefilte fish,
lox, knaidlach, potato kugel and challah.
I'd follow them into that cafeteria
on East Broadway. I'd follow them
into Friedman's on Canal and bite
into blitzes at another table. I'd eat
kasha varnishkes with eggs and listen
to them argue forever
from across the divide.

Almost

I'm sucking chocolate the way my mother
wallowed in the melt and she, though riddled

with anxiety, had the capacity to rise,
to surrender to the succulence.

The green pepper would set off a song.
She'd eulogize the benefits and taste

of an avocado. In abandonment,
she'd scoop the insides out and, for this,

at this moment I almost say thanks
and an "almost" to my father,

who would praise the fat of a sirloin
where the flavor could be found,

and how he scorned anyone who would
cut it away. He recalled the only memory

of his father, who deserted the family
but left that crunch of a cucumber

in my father's ear. The chew and crackle
implanted a distant and present

sound, a more innocuous remnant
of his past and mine. My father would

consume a corn beef on rye, followed by a pastrami on rye, followed by a
tongue on rye, followed by two frankfurters drenched in sauerkraut.

He searched the Bronx for a sour, a truly sour pickle.
The shells of sunflower seeds formed pyramids after

he cracked them open. The ingredients supplied
a satisfying taste and what proved to be

a futile attempt to heal his heart,
a remedy my mother read about along with

fresh cherries that cured arthritis.
She'd often sing *the whiter the bread*

the sooner you're dead and despite the walls
between us, I'd hum along

with her melodic warnings.

The First Stripper or Where Is Jeffrey?

His family lived in the ground floor
apartment. His room looked out at

the street and a few of us would watch
him cuddle his Chihuahua on the windowsill.

It was his stage, showcase. Jeffrey always seemed
to be grinning, especially when he danced

a slow strip tease. His hairless genitals
swayed to a pre-pubescent tune.

Not that I was that interested but I did wonder
if the impulse came from heaven or hell.

One day I was playing in his apartment.
I don't remember the game. His father

returned home, opened the door in a loosened tie,
strolled up to his son and smacked him

across the face. Then said, "What did you do today?"
Jeffrey's smile, almost faded, like leftovers,

stranded remains. I had no questions or
explanations, though more stunned than Jeffrey.

His mother wasn't home. I remember her name
was Barbara. Barbara looked like Doris Day

but with a darker complexion. Unlike Doris
I don't remember her ever smiling

but Jeffrey found the perfect platform
to entertain, to strip to the rhythm

of passing cars and kids who took time-out
from playing marbles, off-the-curb and stickball

to watch . . . and watch

A Request

*Tennessee Williams
at the American Academy, May 23, 1969* (photo)

—Fred W. McDarrah, *Anarchy, Protest, and Rebellion:
And the Counterculture That Changed America* (p.158)

Tennessee Williams looks to his left;
our eyes shift to the right.
The gaze of a skeptic.
Is he glancing at Ruth Stephen or beyond?
His tie swerves. Uneven creases on his forehead,
his left cheek in shadow.
It's the side of the cheek
I kissed . . . oh, no,
it was the left side of the neck.
When I told him I acted in his plays,
he asked, "Where, in class?"
I said yes and then Tennessee
asked, "Why the hair?" My friend Wally
explained: "Paul is in the play *Lenny.*"
Tennessee turned his head slightly,
said, "Kiss me,"
pointing to the spot;
I aimed my lips
for Laura,
for Tom,
for Blanche . . . her wounds,
for Amanda;
I planted the kiss for Stanley,
for Brick and that click
he welcomed when he drank.
I kissed him for the Bronx I deserted
but like St. Louis for Tom
we were both drawn back.
I kissed him because he asked me.
I kissed him for a play
he hadn't written yet.

Nonjudgmental

Sidney Carroll and Conrad Janis
with a George Segal sculpture at the Sidney Janis gallery,
15 East 57th Street, Sept 23, 1966 (photo)

—Fred W. McDarrah, *Anarchy, Protest, and Rebellion:*
And the Counterculture That Changed America (p. 107)

There's the backside of a sculpture:
two figures intimately
on top of one another.
A sculpture of a man
with arms crossed
watches a few feet away
while three actual humans
look at the lens—and we too
are voyeurs. The sculptures, white
with wrinkles that papier-mâché
or clay often create.
Like certain works of art, it gets
better the more we examine it,
even the embarrassment
of the guy in a bow tie who denies
the aesthetics of copulation:
Perhaps the figure lying down is dead,
Perhaps the one on top is also dead.
Perhaps they are ghosts or soiled angels.
On Sheridan Square in the West Village,
a George Segal sculpture of
a man relaxes on a bench;
I would sit beside this friend
and recite my sordid stories.
His unflinching countenance
listening, and listening.

Empty

In a March Against Death:
A Vietnam Memorial, a display of coffins
is placed in front of the White House,
November 15, 1969. (photo)

—Fred W. McDarrah, *Anarchy, Protest, and Rebellion:*
And the Counterculture That Changed America (p. 54)

The caskets in a line,
ten white ones,
the same color
as the house
in the background,
sitting with its arms
spread and you can't
blame the White House.
Oh I guess you can
but you can't blame
Robert Swift in the first casket,
Robert, who tried to show
off in high school,
dribbling between
his legs, a sure way not to make the team.
Finally, he wears a uniform;
he hasn't started to decay.
In the second box is
Richard Finke, who brought
the tallest sugar cane to class:
he carried it back from Cuba
when Cuba was a friend.
In the next is Nicky Pizzano,
who interceded
when I was being pummeled
by the school maniac.
His raspy
voice floats

out of the coffin,
and again repeats
my name with alarm.

I Don't Want to Turn an Accident into a Poem but when

he flips over the gray Honda,
leaving his bicycle and lands,
his middle-aged body
remains face down.
I pull to the side,
dial 911 from there
to the Fire department
then on hold
hold
and a voice
warns me not to
move him and
I tell him not to move
and he asks why and I explain
the laws of physics are in action,
force exerted by object one upon object two is equal in magnitude and opposite in direction to the force exerted by object two upon object one, particularly at the point of contact
where it puffs and expands into a discolored sphere. I don't want to look at, but someone holds his hand now, an expert in CPR. The bike rider doesn't know
what happened
or where he is
but I memorized
the cross section at
Rose and Walgrove
Rose and Walgrove,
Rose and Walgrove
I repeat to the lady on the line.
And I don't want to bring up Bette
because I don't want to drag this further
into sentiment,
into common bicycle grease
into the muck of body debris
but for that second
when he flew in the air,
for that second,
Bette lived again
and died again.

Breeze

Finger cymbals
on Fifth Avenue By Hare Krishna
Aug 2, 1969 (photo)

—Fred W. McDarrah, *Anarchy, Protest, and Rebellion:*
And the Counterculture That Changed America (p. 118)

They might show up on your street,
swaying in a trance beyond the grip of self.
They catch you on any corner
and serenade and I too would
like to be enclosed in a song:
a place without all the asking
and reaching. I might shave
my head, tap a drum or shake
a cymbal; let the breeze run up my robe.
Let years roll on as we orbit,
never thinking of fame, mental institutions,
the cower of my mother. Just
the encasement, the breathing.

Slow Return

*Tomkins Square Park,
10th Street and Avenue A,
Feb 13, 1964* (photo)

—Fred W. McDarrah, *Anarchy, Protest, and Rebellion:
And the Counterculture That Changed America* (p. 67)

Covered with snow,
the swerving walkway,
semicircles and bare trees.
Stripped, weather beaten,
a people-less photo,
a eulogy to the park, minus
concerts, murders, gangs,
homeless—and the celebrations.
Allen Ginsberg lived on its border,
the 10th street side.
Kristen Linkleter, a voice teacher,
walked on my back in her ground floor
apartment on the Avenue B side.
We weren't intimate, the park and I,
until I collapsed on its bench,
coming down
from LSD.
It was then it held me in its bosom,
rocked me between A and B,
softly chanting: *You belong.
Sit as long as you like—
until the trees are trees;
the leaves, leaves,
and people, just people—
until everything
settles back
into its name.*

Sarah Maclay

Nightfall Marginalia (What Books Press), a 2023 Foreword INDIES Finalist in Poetry, is Sarah Maclay's fifth collection. Her poems and essays, supported by a Yaddo residency and a City of Los Angeles Individual Artist Fellowship and awarded the *Tampa Review* Prize for Poetry and a Pushcart Special Mention, among other honors, have appeared in *APR, FIELD, Ploughshares, The Tupelo Quarterly, The Writer's Chronicle, The Best American Erotic Poetry: From 1800 to the Present, Poetry International*, where she served as Book Review Editor for a decade, and many other publications, and she was the artistic director of The 3rd Area, a gallery-based reading series in DTLA and Bergamot Station, that ran for several years.

Her "Fugue States Coming Down the Hall," a piece for stage, appears in the Kostelanetz anthology *Scenarios: Scripts to Perform*, and was presented at Oberlin College and at Beyond Baroque, in Venice, where she offers periodic workshops. Several of her poems, the basis of the album *Identity Had Gone*, were set to a classical score by Kostas Rekleitis. She has taught creative writing at USC and, for nearly two decades, at LMU, and also offers private workshops, while roaming between LA and her native Montana, where she has also performed as a singer/songwriter. Her work has been translated into Spanish and Macedonian. Her fourth chapbook, *The H.D. Sequence—A Concordance*, was published by Walton Well in 2024.

A Breathing Lake

Above us, floating in the dark
like opened lanterns—

as the water's onyx sheen
closes to opaque:

lotuses, where stars would be.

How we wanted to eat them
with our eyes.

How we almost did.

So much closer now that we could almost pull them
toward us like austere balloons.

All around, our stillness, our suspension.

A Mirror of Leaves

Even now, I draw you toward me—
Even as the black mold furs the ceiling,
Spanish moss hanging abruptly from the walls,
Draping across the furniture—that Rococo fauteuil and my settee—
In dry organic antimacassars and ratty doily strands
While the edges of the Aubusson carpet, still beneath us, are sipped—
By silverfish and rug beetles and moths and the curtains
Blow into the room, along with the graying leaves of autumn,
Already dead, already light as termites, thin as ash—
And still, your chest is an open door
And birds fly out
Of the vaulted ceiling of your cathedral heart
Like red origami
And tiny white—fly, they fly into the wild air
Of the room as you tiptoe toward me
In your gray mime, like a shadow
As alive as trees
While I gently pull on the long green strand of yarn
As it gathers into a ball
I can hold in my hand, and some would say
I cry red tears or that
My entire chest is as red as my waist-length uncut hair
And that it seems I can only stare straight ahead as I weep
And pull your open heart
Toward mine, even as this island of wool below us
Diminishes as I perch my stool upon it,
Oblivious to the ragged, shrinking edges,
As the invisible choir of insects
Erodes the original design.
And some would say: so focused am I on the wool in my hand
That I don't even notice the growing devastation
Of the room
But I must tell you
—And you can see this for yourself if you look closely—
That the lines descending from my eyes are not tears, no,
Or even blood—not now—

But merely the last of the remaining gold leaf
Etched into these walls in the 18th century
In another climate—
Barely visible now: a blanched, infested background.
And others do not recognize or know, I guess,
The way the skin can rouge in pleasure—
But mine always does—
And though I know I'm facing the other direction
And shouldn't be able to see this,
If you look yourself, you'll find
That the mirror above the fireplace clearly reflects
The gathering clouds that have entered the room
In a gusty rush of nimbus further darkening the chalky
Charcoal look of the crown moldings
And below the mantel, where the fire should be,
Or at least a screen: a massive nest of webs.
Yet even as everything around us grows gradually
Colourless and intermittently devoured
I can feel you coming toward me, though I can't yet see
The exact features of your face. Your step is light;
Your balance precise and honed as a wooden marionette
Freed of all strings, yet—miraculously—choosing to keep in your heart
This one bit of yarn
As I hold and roll the other end
And as I hand you, finally, this small green ball—
This homespun ball of my waiting—
A bird will fly out of your chest into mine,
And the joined cathedral of our twinned hearts
Will be our sanctuary—sanctuary enough—
Vast enough, unending—
And as this infusion of color you've given me
As I have welcomed you,
Even though the room itself grows nearly tarnished, leached
Of hue, drawn down
To a bleached-out play of values and some drafty chiaroscuro
While the weather and bugs peel the paint and even silently lick
The stains from the corners of the wood and burrow through the cornices—
As this color you've managed to preserve in me
—At some sacrifice to yours, I'd say—seeps back now,

Also, into you,
And my gaze shifts from the task of attending to this yarn
To the proper study of your features—
Because, finally, home is simply an article of faith,
An article of mirror; of mirroring—
As your features become clearer, light unbends
The chambers and the hallways of the cathedral
In which it's as though we've really always lived—
And, even now, can't fathom.
And even in this moment of a room's final unraveling,
This one's no illusion
As it opens into the new, unfolding architecture of our future—
Solid and unfinalfied, unformed.

—after Remedios Varo's "Les Feuilles Mortes"

Real State

Thou shalt hang thy blankets from a tree

or thou shalt score a gig as a retail doorman on Rodeo

Thou shalt cover thyself with a sheet of clear plastic and kick at the corner of Broadway and 6th, while pedestrians pass

Thou shalt fumble for keys at the end of the night shift, still in scrubs

Thou shalt hang a right in thy pre-owned 911 Carrera

Thou shalt remove all personal belongings from thy cubicle before the end of the business day. Here's a box.

Thou shalt spring for the 27-thousand-dollar beaded gown not far from the Bois d'Argent

Thou shalt prop the mattress against the eucalyptus across the street from the house in escrow, the two-story for lease, and the reno covered in Tyvek

Thou shalt park thine SLK 320 under the sycamore leaves

Thou shalt not be able to light your cigarette in the wind as you sit on the stoop behind the open storefront display of wighead mannequins

It's an economy storage box

Thou shalt pick up the tab on the ornamental 13-thousand-dollar Buddha and that 6K bottle of scotch in the duty-free

Thou shalt dry thy clothes on the guardrail in front of the Walgreen's and Shabu-Shabu

Thou shalt walk with weights in the evening as the sky turns amethyst then amber and the water comes on, inches from the rusty grass

Drive 45 on the boulevard

Thou shalt leave the couch and the plastic plant on the curb at the end of the month

Thou shalt load the Relo Cube for pickup at Glyndon and Vienna

Thou shalt live in the back of a 1950s Buick with shattered glass

You can use the wi-fi at the Starbucks next to the Dollar Loan

Thou might get a construction job on the northern side of the National Rent-A-Fence

Thou shalt put the tents up after the shoppers leave

Thou shalt no longer be able to afford the unpermitted room within earshot of gunshot and helicopter

Thou shalt "join the 17 million readers who have fallen"

Thou shalt try to sleep in the late afternoon at the base of a streetlamp on the hidden side of a Shell in the Marina

Thou shalt lose thy shirt selling armor, rugs, and chandeliers

No Parking Any Time

Thou shalt stick two signs in the lawn: "house for lease" and "tutoring"

Thou shalt check the stats on the listings from the last six days

Thou shalt organize thy belongings carefully under the overpass

Thou shalt not vacate the premises without giving a 30-day notice

Thou shalt guard the tents at Venice & Globe

Open door policy

Thou shalt not sleep except upon a concrete floor

After Vuillard

House is a dappled construct
House is a shadowed land on a small hill
House is before the abundant garden—
The birdlike stems and butterflies
Of flowers pirouetting,
Nearly as large as the windows,
Or leaves like yellow diurnal bats
House is behind the woman in the satin pink kimono,
Face as large as the first floor
House is the tiny gardener,
Head as big as a rose,
Inspecting the hedge
Perspective is filigreed blue shadow
Below the white hibiscus, stamens
Longer than a hand
Windows turning red as the roof in the evening sun,
Red as the tallest floribunda
Is the woman with rose-petal hair
In the lattice of shadows, handing—
Is the dark canoe-shaped shadow on the roof
The figure behind the open curtain
The closed cerulean shutters—
Their slightly aged pastel, the texture of their rough wood
The door thrown open
The hot sweet smell of summer-singed pollen
The soft sounds of garments landing on the floor
Is for sale
Is her blue hat
Is the cracked tectonic floor
Is no longer there
Is the sun hitting the pavers, the terraced, dry dirt steps,
The chair
The thorns
Perspective is the removed corset
Longer than petals
The flying light

The light flying
Night coming on, to the left
Above the acacia, below the pine
Illuminating the chorus line of genies
Playing their bagpipes
As the cannas and the ultimate dwarf bearded irises
Unfurl, unravel, nearly ragged, vulvic, utterly,
And the whole yard is full of flying things
Abundantly tethered enough to stay in position
For a time
For this moment
The blue, I'm telling you, I can't make out
Though it's closer to larkspur than indigo,
Closer to denim, closer to bamboo
I guess I should be happy
How does it speak?

—after 'The Garden at Vaucresson'

It Is Not a Bridge

The bed　　　　red　　　wood　　with scrolls　　　　—along the side, black ink—

the bed　　　or the coffin　　　above the river—　　　the water filled with bats —

　　　or　　　　birds—

I stand on it—　　　　　　on top of the red　　　wood　　　bed　　　above the river

in wind—　　　　my hair—long, black—　　　and all of the layers of my clothes—

swirling in wind like some cubist kimono　　　　—the swirling squares of my robes

and maybe the blankets　I am now standing in　　　as I raise my white sword—

my sword, my reed　　—my quill—　　　long　　　white　　　yellow

—as I raise my long sword　　　toward the fish　　　above my head

riding my sleeve like a sleigh, like a basket—　　　riding my sleeve

like a silk bassinette　　　—that whiskerfish　　　ready to jump in the water

before I fall　　　　　before I strike—

Rehearsal for Ending

Feathers—
or birds, or leaves

fell slowly into the snow
among the dark thin hounds

and their hunters,
obscuring the wet bark torsos

of the trees,
larger

even than the black-clad
skaters on celadon

ponds, grim as the
morning sky

and melting as,
seconds later,

snow—I'm sure—was floating up—
flakes or white feathers

losing their scant
gravity

as the ice began to burn
along the edges

and the drifts of tulle,
veiling the long grass—

already slowed, elongated—
tangled in muddy clouds of web

as Mahler appeared—
I think it was Mahler

—or something had happened to the air,

echoing the distance among those same
increasing shades of green, in notes

or in what trembles—

something else, something far apart

as the roiling gray of a fishtail-
braided cloud, years

and seconds later

in that pentimento of rain,
grainy and dark

and darkening the distances of green
waters and murky fields

until it seems barely possible to make out
the few abandoned fishing boats

and almost impossible to tell
whether the two tall stalks

are cut-off sails
or the edges of self-pruning cottonwoods

that have grown, in confusing weathers,
up through salt

and through the teal and emerald of
the slippery reeds of shore toward the roiling gray corn

of the clouds in their horizontal twisting above shards of wall
below. And then white moths,

like motes, floating into the star-dark sky,
just as after the box is opened and things fly out

some of them are still alive, and light,
even as the sail-cloak darkens over the body

and the lover extends the fingers again toward the wound, and tries,
and cannot stand.

Hunger

The slip was not satin, but poppy.
A linen sky gone pale and the long
cascading drapes and walls that same cool white
but the cypress, its fallen needles, the rooftops
were umber, the fence, the beginning of night:
small, invisible cries, and like a wing that wooden
fence grew large with shadow as its shape
entered the window, umber,
amber bulbs exposed below
the flaring black shade,
plump with filament, lit, pendulous
and, it seemed, beginning to rise
as the languor of too many months-without-end—
enforced, unnatural languor—
had gathered, like silk, into the crack of thigh
against bent knee, the seam of fleshy upper arm,
crease of elbow, the mystery
of triangle made by the shade of red cloth fallen high over leg,
the shape the covered nipples made as the breasts splayed
to balance a hand flung backward, out of sight and
into foreshadowing, into the scent of the ganja filling the hallway
—nearly strong as skunk—curving its way below the door and into the room
through the rough-hewn gap where light crept through at night
across the closed face, brow held tight as scar above the nose,
kohled eyes focused by a dust mote on the floor or the inner
lip of the terracotta urn.
Scent of sugar, sweat, tobacco seeping through the old pipes,
clinging to the pillows like a second skin.
Galangal nights. Arpeggiated dawn.
Empty Newport pack on the hellstrip.
Mind like ribbons. Leather bangs.
Time beyond girdle, the giving up,
the belly abundant, the giving in,
again, again, again, again, again.

Before Us

There is a mauve photographic bowl of rain
                —though some would say a cup
A sultry plague before the fandango of alleys
An armament / arm / armband tossed into the gray / the grim Corvette
        at the rehearsal of velour and anise / ankle / anklet
A muzzle of parched starlings sleeping like geckos / geishas / geese
                      just lounging
        after the Sabbath of compromised kilt / kin / kiln
(I'm certain about the alleys and the alliances)
(I'm certain of the colour, of the bowl)
And did I mention that huddle of parrots? Yes. Five, green.
                Clustered near the beige of the third-floor windows.
After the honcho / the hole, the whole damn holiday opens
                and the dam spills into the castanets of the waiting hand.
And it's here the maraca ticks like a rattlesnake on a short leash.
(I'm certain of the Geiger counter, the saber /
      the stomping / the sticking.)
And the compensation—it's worthwhile.
There's a moan in the attic, and one in the basement,
A twisting / tweaking / twerking in the den.
To be clear—did I say that the bowl is the size of a valley?
And did I mention this rush is the colour of mauve?
           (As the rehearsal-velour deliquesces to velvet—
                  velvet dissolving into the smooth vernacular of fur . . .)
There's a cat / a catch in the breath at the edge of the bed in the lush
      hush of morning,
a slant / a sliver / a sip of new light in the palms.
I'm certain of the armature of nothing . . .
as I'm certain that the husk has cracked, its scraps concussed.
There's a flamenco that rustles the edges of rust and of dusk and of morning,
that rattles the dust from the corridors of musk:
      this is its cusp
(as the licorice Pernods, as socks bloom into paisley stockings,
        as dawn's viridian muddle of leaves becomes a nest of trust
            and armbands / guns are garters—inveterate, seated deep,
I'm certain of the moaning, the anemone, the memory,

the tangle and the tango and the glow—
as I'm certain of the shade, of this blueberry-vermillion.
And of the green parrots, I am certain.
Certain.)

Holaday Mason

Holaday Mason sixth collection of poetry, *As If Scattered*, was published by Giant Claw Press in 2024. She is the author of *Towards the Forest, Dissolve, The Red Bowl: A Fable in Poems, The "She" Series: A Venice Correspondence* (with Sarah Maclay), *The Weaver's Body* and two chapbooks—*Interlude* and *Light Spilling From its Own Cup*. A Pushcart nominee, her publications include *Hotel Amerika, Spillway, Pool,* and *Poetry International*. Frequently anthologized and a finalist for the Dorset prize, Ms. Mason has served as poetry editor of *Mental Shoes* and *Furious Pure*, as well as coeditor for *Echo 681*, an anthology from Beyond Baroque where she has led the Wednesday Night Workshop, as well as several generative writing events. In private practice as a psychotherapist since 1993, she is also a photographer, orchestrating surrealistic scenes that underscore the mysteries of aging and being a part of the natural world.

So, What if the Chimes Are Silent?

1

It is Sunday. Look how the tiny
unnamed brown birds in the pomegranate
shudder, so small they'd fit together
in my palms, yet they shake the entire tree.

See how the shady side of the fountain
has gathered moss so thick it might be
clay one could mold into a strong vessel.

It's always a surprise, how the yellow rose
vines, rising from barren root,
claw, thorn & bud over the neighbor's wall
(the one who's never liked me),
until flowers consume the redwood fence

the way you wrapped around me
& together we become an original
carved from old scars. My red
cup balances in the dirt, steam weaves
from coffee in the orbit of morning.

You quietly play the crooked guitar
so don't see me point to a knot of seagulls
crossing the split-open nectarine clouds,

spider webs loosely drift through
the budding red maple until the gulls
part into three, unite, part, unite
again, caught in some invisible airstream,

the way prayer sounds into & through,
the way just sitting with you in
the dawn & plaiting your hair seems
everything one needs to stay alive.

2

My red cup balances

in the dirt.

Yellow roses

vine the morning,

claw

through old scars.

Caught

in some invisible

airstream,

the sun crests the roofline,

alive.

And Both of Us Saw Tiny Spears of Violet

    1

He is red ripples
on the gentle hills.
Undulations
of antique vistas.
A sky of winter.
An almost spring sky.
Next season.
Then to the next.
We might lose our way,
may fail, but we're going
anyhow, towards blossoms
cascaded over the castings
of the hills. As if
smeared. As if scattered.
Moments you can't make up.
I never had sweet dreams.
But this one is. And sure,
I know one should not
remove the wooden stake
from the frozen heart,
we're risking total
collapse, but fuck it,
we do it anyhow. Threads
of violets release from the throats
of all involved in a kind of howling
that's bearable, as if a curse
has been lifted. Not everything
has to be lovely, yet this is.
There is ruby all over
the landscape. We could be
anywhere. It doesn't matter
who thinks what.
We are home because
we woke up & we said so.

2

Antique vistas

smear all the hills.

We could be anywhere.

But we're going

anyhow,

howling.

Beauty

The old hound dog stands bowlegged
in the meadow
befuddled by butterflies
tying the spring air in knots.

They have bewitched him
as only love or beauty can.

And when the two white cranes land near the forest pond,

it will be too much.
He may try to bite

the sunlight from the sky,
the colors from the flowers,
the stripes from the bees.

He may run in circles,
then try to hide his nose.

He may need some help.
We may need some too.

Shrine

I knead your hip and thigh
with the heels of my hands
in the rhythm of making
legato, adagio, the smell
of you swelling in the fire.

As the piano is built.
As the horehound frosts, spreading
the lace mantilla over the lower
fields. Rise into me. *Pianissimo.*
You will never starve.

Fire

You never expected her to burst naked, flying from the tree
        & not a neon billboard in sight to direct you
so you must stay the course of nocturnal beauty.
      ~

The back of a running doe is a wave
        threading through high grass—exactly the way
the woman's spine is, as each minute is & you want the whole
      ~

pale length of her, from crown to cave—her skin sheet
        a sail beneath which all else is shadow—
shadow bodies everywhere, waiting to meet—but *you* knew that.
      ~

And, much the way the doe remains forever standing in the road—
        such is the woman's slow motion leap
as if from a fire, those dried leaves, amber confetti,
      ~

dripping into the dark around her body
        while the unmade bed of her red
hair swells, then nearly sweeps the broken yellow lines
      ~

of the highway where *you* stand so far below. She reaches
        farther & harder than you could ever
bear, her might in the tips of fingers saturated
      ~

with what? *You* don't know, but your *body* does
        because it feels her body flinging out between
the ground & the sky, a pale weaver suspended
      ~

& not a single hint of starlight—
no, she alone cuts her own white country open.

Menopause

The pause of the blood, the not now
or ever impasse of womb, iron of emptiness,
the buried plasma roots of beginning,
the end of the eggs, the un-union of skin,
the played-out tryst, the staunched
memory, stolen heirloom, scarred
slit wrist, the un-hatched, un-cried,
dried blown-out wisp of smoke, the sealed eye,
silenced tome, floating black fish,
un-made unmade bed, the cessation
of red, the blank rivulet, the witch's song
inside the deaf nest—   ten young
drowning men in the surf. One on his belly,
a newborn clinging to his back, screaming.

Prism

And the next day at noon, under a tree, I balance a meal on my knees
& watch midsummer leaves fall, quivering like furred caterpillars
in the grass under the cut velvet lace of shade.
One of the dead comes to sit at my right hip, explaining the facts
of forgiveness, distinct from grief, which, like trouble,
must be culled from clinging to things. My brother dead
at fifty-six with such suede brown eyes & now, the crushed organ
between my thin ribs hammering as I sit longing so badly for his smell.
I offer rice. He declines. *Unraveling is not unworthy of love*, he says,
exactly the way the life of music comes undone in the moment
a note flares alive, exactly like a curving candle flame, each shifting
particle dying & birthing at once. Today, between my legs is the sweet aching
stamp of a man not seen for months, who washed up with the moon-tide,
coming inside the moment the round black & white clock, (whose face
was turned to the mirror) reflected the seconds back onto themselves perfectly.
Then on an arrow fine point of focus, his body, each touch, began & ended
its own arc, burning holy as australis borealis, strangely rare, no matter
how familiar the hue. My mouth told my heart in a dream to build
a wedding dress of my own skin. In broad daylight the ghost knows how
badly I failed, how badly he himself failed, how sorry, sorry sad the hungers
of lost children. In the sunlight, the tiered fountain's droplets,
split into bracelets of light, veils of elementals locked in union, like these
men, who've left some of themselves inside me—plus one sweet black butterfly
bruise on my inner arm, a blue tiger in the clock—purring. The dead one
begins to smile as if breaking the sound barrier. He's traveling all over & all at once
has decided to take a bite of my bean soup—the spoon now playing the inside
of the clay bowl in a little clink, clink symphony, exactly in that same slow way
dawn collects our names through the dark hours, cradling us all in the pearled
petals of our dreams. A flea bites my ankle. I am a tambourine
under this tissue sky. At noon, the moon waxing, until tomorrow,
is abiding with the others, on the other side of earth, in the other day
or is it the next day or is it this same day, but midnight? I remember to shiver.
I shiver blue love talking to the dead one whose eyes remain the color I recall.
I waltz the spoon given music of this noon meal, alone with the imprint of one man
in my cunt, another in the grave—my flesh, a wrinkling silk dress, some
shimmering skin a snake might gradually shake off, iridescent as moonstone

or water, not just how bones are flutes & dust is heaven, not that, but
how Being floats over & within the specifics, how the body is the bowl & the rice—
serpent & water—echoing cave inside of which I find you again & again—brothers,
lovers, beloveds, all of us are there—here, always & at once . . . listen!
Can you hear? Can you hear?

The Edge of the World

I offer you a small peeled orange and say,
This is the earth.

The Irish moss, quiet

As a caterpillar, tempts
You to dig your feet into its wool
And loose its scent.

Our naked limbs in the sun, we
Impress ourselves into each other,

Bear the unbearable light.

Here, before the dark cold of the room
Where the man who has your face dies,

We remain
The sole witnesses as a single moth,
(A strange and barely blue one) seals itself to the window

Where it writes—*We can't help who
We love.*

Neptune Chorale

      1

I have always had a weakness
for beautiful dresses of flora—

dusky silks, eyelet cottons—
a closet of cravings
no longer needed.

The floors have grown
so hard tonight, doorknobs
gleam pewter & stormy
as if to say *age can't be tidy.*

Your face—a planet
above me in a lake of night.

Rare rain scores the roof,
curves & scratches against
the windows but I've
drawn a strange horizon.

The storm can't get inside
the ring of beginning—

where we have time,
we still have
a little time left.

2

I no longer quite gleam,

have a weakness

for the storm

the beautiful curves,

& scratches of beginnings—

Operas can't be tidy.

Highway 99

You downshift into the yam heat.
In the valley of grapevines
we don't talk of childlessness.
Your elbow is a wing in the open window
as a confetti of leaves and shadows
rushes by. I know you've never seen
these orchards in spring bloom—
how the pink lanterns of light float down.
Red potatoes lie on the ground now,
the color of dried blood.
I make the sign of the cross.
The Kings River smells of drowned cattle.
Then Exitor, Pixley, terra bella, sweet dirt
all around as faithful to the sky
as water is to gravity. In Delano, sweethearts
will wait past midnight, when heat
like a camel carries them to each other.
Your left shoulder is burning.
with the setting sun, I sleep and dream
there is a family by the roadside
dressed in Easter clothes. Abeula. Mama.
The father's good Panama hat points brim down
under the car's yawning hood
as the smallest girl's red dress
opens like a tulip. She holds a grace
of white blossoms, loco weed,
bridal bouquet. I reach for her.
I reach for you. In a swarm,
battling ants cross and re-cross
her two best shoes. Behind her,
sunflowers snake through the barbed wire.
I dream I give you a palm full of almond blossoms.
I dream of tumbleweeds, divining rods
and soil. When I wake it isn't Easter after all.
Still, we have to go to church.
Take what we can harvest.

Towards the Forest
after Edvard Munch, 1915

There are footprints in the grass:
Crushed clover.

And the evergreens are etched
With black birds and bone twigs.

It is still a warm season.

The plan is this—

You're strong and you hold me

Until either the moon breaks in two
Or a last snow falls-

Whichever comes first.

I'll return your kiss

Then walk to the bear

Knowing his clear stone eyes

Are as dark as every ending
That will breathe across our faces.

Tracing his teeth with my fingers

His fur will be my bed.

Then I'll long for you as for no other

And it will be so quiet.

From the Mountain to the Prairie to the Oceans, White With Foam
—*Irving Berlin 1918*

My mother comes out of the darkness.
The tunnel is red, is opening, closing
like a wild poppy tracking day into night.
Under the floating indigo mountains,
there are no words, just this act as she pulses out
with her mother's black & white checkered apron
tied around her, sagging slightly as if the pockets
are full of peanuts or keys & she intends something.
I know this since her lips are moving—not unlike
a silent player piano in an empty formal dining room,
the table set with tarnished silver, no, there's no
discernable sound, only a slight humming
from the diagrams of history's shadows—
too many to count flinging from her chest
as she steps onto the black highway.

You check your watch to see where you are standing.
The sound is everywhere without sound, like a lie
you can glimpse, like a city of ether yet built of solids,
of minerals, of soils. We are running out of sand.
A child in another time shrieks, *everybody, don't see me!*
stridently, over & over. What will become of us
we wonder & search for each other's hands, closing
our fingers around one another like wild red poppies
clinging as we watch the indigo peaks fade.

There is a small deer at the edge of the copse
that has burrowed through the blackberry hedge
following a tunnel carved into the bramble wall
by many years of animals leading one another
to the ragged border of the cottonwoods, that maze
now winter-bare behind the doe, who sniffs
the water-laden atmosphere startling only slightly

as a car sluices past speeding on the wounded
spine of asphalt & she finds nothing new
under the pewter sun, just a humming, a dappling.

My mother swells like roses in her bell white gown,
turns on the bathroom light & never returns.
Bells ring in cathedrals & dells everywhere at once,
calling out the names of immense stones sawn in half,
ancestries etched in every single tone. As we watch her go,
no one calls out, calls her back—we do not dare startle
the veils—our breath like sleds gliding so tenderly
over the air that opens the seams of the earth invisibly.
We hear a dog in the distance squeal in some sort of terror
or pain but we cannot reach out to comb its coat
gently with our palms. We have to hold on.
There seems no other way, or regret might gather
in a sea of black pebbles filling our throats & genitals.

Frozen, we bear witness as the indigo mountains
are carried away in the beaks of so many crows
like memories of something pure, truthful, until
the sky becomes a bed of spilled ink, a babbling roar,
drowning, not brave & costly like all true freedoms.
Goodbye, we wave to the saturated peaks, as the doe
comes to stand beside us, staring at our locked hands,
then our wet feet covered in sticks & mud, then
at our faces—searching our eyes as if asking what color
the future is, asking like a fingerprint, or music.
She studies, wearing the same wordlessly quizzical look
I'd last seen my mother wear when in the island house
when she'd come to kneel with great pain at my side where
I'd slept on the floor near the fire & whispered,
Did you do the right thing? Do you still believe
that's true? Then the kettle was screaming, which
simply meant it was time to go.

Jim Natal

Jim Natal is the author of five poetry collections, most recently *Spare Room: Haibun Variations* and *52 Views: The Haibun Variations*. His previous collections include *Memory and Rain, Talking Back to the Rocks,* and *In the Bee Trees*, which was a finalist for the PEN American and Publisher's Marketing Association Ben Franklin awards. He has also penned six chapbooks. A multi-year Pushcart Prize nominee, his poetry has been published in *Spillway, Hotel Amerika, San Pedro River Review, Alligator Juniper, Los Angeles Review* and *Hayden's Ferry Review*, among other journals, and in many anthologies, among them, *New Poets of the American West*.

Widely featured as a reader at festivals, colleges, and bookstores across the country, Natal, with his wife Tania Baban, a graphic designer, founded Conflux Press in 2003. He served as founder and director of Hassayampa Institute's The Literary Southwest at Yavapai College in Prescott, Arizona, after serving as a co-founder, curator and host of The Rose Café series in Venice, CA, and PoemX in Santa Monica, as well as helping to establish a multi-genre writing series at Antioch University, where he earned his MFA. He has taught writing at Yavapai and Prescott colleges. He lives in Marina del Rey.

Reading Lao Tzu, Sun Mountain, Santa Fe
for Don Campbell

It was time, and Sun Mountain
massed closer than ever. A trail to a clearing
bounded by boulders, *piñones* sticky with
beads of sap, loose scree and cholla to
keep me alert, a sage-scented place painted
in quick thick incandescent strokes.

A lizard crept from a cleft near my boot,
eyed me and my small book sideways,
decided a creature sitting so still, awash
in the Tao like a river rock in whitewater,
posed no threat. And wasn't the day warm,
the sky high-altitude blue?

On the highway to and from
Albuquerque, spokes joined hubs
to form wheels; the riveted skin of an Airstream
glinted, just a pindot of hard focus in the glare,
sun magnified, incomprehensible, intense,
effort with no effort.

The lizard basked, did push-ups—
such purposeless purpose! Meanwhile,
down on the Plaza and in the outskirt malls,
chasing and acquisition drove humanity mad
until the cooling hours arrived and
simple necessity reasserted itself.

I read, inert as any rarified element, shared
space and breath with my reptile companion.
Things have names but don't need them.
The path is easy if you follow it.
I emptied my cup and stood up.
Got lost on the way back to the car.

Sweet Home Chicago

My hometown is the smell of El train wires in winter,
orange sparks crackling under flurrying skies, brakes
screeching around buttressed curves like rutting cats
in alleys behind fatback brick apartment buildings, it's
graffiti on wheels, your tongue stuck to the third rail.

Overcast cinder, dinge, and russet dominate, the same
peasant palette as Van Gogh's "The Potato Eaters";
streetlights play the angles of battleship-gray porch slats,
peeling stairs glazed in hip-breaking, shoulder-wrenching
sheet ice. It's a smell that coats the throat in ozone,

that roils up chimneys of nostrils, soots the ceilings
of sinuses, permeates your heaviest clothes more
than blues bar cigarette smoke, guitar-lick midnights,
the rush of stale beer and fumes of disinfectant reek when
the joint's front door cracks the brittle shell of morning.

My home is frozen footprints and the caked corrosion on
sagging bellies of GM hulks, the shudder and grind of
sluggish pistons, iron engine blocks left running to thaw,
spewing blue exhaust perfume while hard water streams
down plastic shower curtains and coffee filters drip.

It doesn't matter what you wear crossing the Michigan
Avenue Bridge in January, the river below cabbage-green as
a bowl of revenge served cold. Coats stuffed with feathers
of geese and ducks are helpless prey, carcasses left
after the wind called "The Hawk" picks them clean.

The smell of my hometown penetrates, pervades like red
stains on butchers' aprons, a meat locker's chill. It's sodden
brown shopping sacks, babushkas, boots, and gloves soggier
than the buns at Al's Beef Stand, the fries at Carl's Hot Dogs,
yellow mustard, sour pickles, pepperoncini on the side.

The smell is chronic, a phantom ache from lugging
50-pound bags of sidewalk salt, shoveling too much
wet snow. It's a heart attack waiting to happen and it's

to the bone, baby, to the bone . . .

The Sense of Touch

The Sense of Touch c. 1615-16 (oil on canvas)

—Jusepe de Ribera (Spanish, 1591-1652)

The blind philosopher in the painting
cradles the back of a sculpted head
as if lifting it from weightless sleep.
With thick fingers he probes
Carrara whorls, cool planes, indentations—
ears, eye hollows, carved clusters of tousled hair—
skims from forehead down bridge of nose,
passing lips that do not whisper clues,
rounds curve of chin to truncated neck,
feels for echoes of ringing hammer blows,
trying to absorb through touch alone
what he might miss if he had sight,
indifferent, perhaps unaware of
the canvas portrait flat beside him on the table.

In the darkness of early morning
I feather my hands over your skin,
caress shoulders, upper arms, cross crevices,
warm fields, lay palms on either side of spine,
read slowly down to dimples of
your lower back deep enough to capture rain.
What, I wonder, would a casual viewer see
so plainly in the foreground that
even with vision and the rising sun
I will never know about you.

Rain in L.A.
Thursday morning

This is a dialogue town,
hard-boiled repartee in a soft-boiled climate.
The mountains wisecrack to the desert,
while the Santa Anas, the red winds,
wring their raspy hands, snivel and sweat
like Peter Lorre waiting for a call from
the ocean on a heavy black phone.
Here, nobody goes out when it rains.
Authors read to the backs of empty chairs.
The movies talk to themselves.
Does the whole city steal
that rare chance to stay home, to listen
to actual weather spackling the windows,
"So What" cued up and playing softly,
to drink and shrink the stack of books
beetled beside the bed? Are they all
afraid of hydroplaning on the 405,
upturned SUVs and jack-knifed trailers,
highway patrol cops in yellow slickers
erecting shrines of flares? Or
do Angelenos think they'll melt
like the wicked witch of the coastal west,
leave nothing but a grounded broom
and a puddle on an empty soundstage as if
it's 1939 in Culver City? Oh, man,
it's raining munchkins and evil clouds
of flying monkeys are tumbling in.

Moses

. . . the blonde and blue-eyed bringer of truth, who will not easily be forgiven.

—B.H. Fairchild

My father told me this story just once, rare for him....
Away at college, Depression-era Virginia.
The days when he wore suits to class and
the dogwood and azaleas bloomed.
It was a Friday night and he was
playing poker on the Sabbath.
Fraternity brothers, beer and white lightning,
also a stranger who kept staring at my father
over the spread fan of cards in his hand. Finally,
my father had enough of the stranger's eyes.
An athlete then, fit and handsome,
he called the stranger's bluff, called him
out, put his cards face up on the table
and challenged, *What are you staring at?*
Did the boy—these were college boys, don't forget—
blink or abruptly stand, the others at the table
perhaps catching the first scent of
rain in the air before the thunder rumbles?
When the boy responded, his words were
whittled from tones of the purest, deepest south.
Are you a Jew? the southern boy asked. Asked.
My father said he was. The boy spoke again.
But, he said, *you don't have any horns.*
The way my father told it, he didn't
punch the boy, though he wanted to. The reason
he didn't fight, my father said, was because
the boy was serious, incredulous, shaken.
All his life this boy had been told that Jews
had horns, like Michelangelo's marble Moses.
And now, face-to-face with his first Jew
in the flesh, the Jew had nothing

on his head, not even a yarmulke.
My father stopped his story there, did not
describe the other boy or mention if he ever
saw him again. Was he dirty blonde and lanky,
Adam's apple protruding from a banded collar,
shoulders braced by suspenders?
No, that would be too easy, a stereotype.
Was the boy the first from his family to ascend
to college, a good possibility then.
And what, I wonder, did the southern boy do
that night after the game broke up
and the stone tablets became his?
Did he brood on the mountain,
carry the weight forever in silence,
a holy rage repressed? Or
did he take it down to his people,
go home and topple the idol,
this boy of gold now fallen himself?
And I, in my own college haze,
did not think to ask my father,
Why are you telling me this? Why now?
Never expecting that it would be
the first and only time.

Saguaro Motel

Most of the saguaros are just standing ribs
and my screen door barely strains the sun.
Faded is the primary color, though the dust makes
everything look muted pastel. Except the light,
which is harsh, throwing every dent and edge,
every crease and pore, into razor relief.
There's none of that limpid Hollywood
dreamy creamy margarita afternoon glow.
It's straight tequila's unblinking cheap burn,
because, in this place, light and heat are the same.
The only destination is just passing through.
People hardly stay long enough to sweat the sheets.
Saw the sign out front, they say. *Liked the name*,
they say—(*retro*) (*kitschy*) (*cute*). Then they
register for one night, duck outside to retrieve
forgotten numbers on their out-of-state plates.
I don't know when it slipped by or if
it ever made a stop; a train in the night
with lights in all the windows but one.
It could be worse, I guess. I close the blinds by day,
open them at dusk. The weeks pass in clusters,
like the trucks. I've got my TV dish out back so
I keep up, remind myself each night at 10
why I'm here.

Tree of Life Hotel

Stark against the stark Wisconsin prairie, a hologram
of brick, four stories above a gateless crossing
passed by trains, heading north, going south.

Floors branch from swayback stairways, halls
extending to terminal buds of rooms and baths.

The fire escape clings like iron ivy,
long dead, still rooted to its host.

How many coupled cars have been counted from
how many windows fogged with frost or condensation?

How many hands have perched on sooty sills,
paint peeling like bark, in how many sleeveless Augusts?

How many fitful sleepers have stirred, half-heard
whistles stretch into the night, pulled along
like fallen leaves beside the rusting rails?

Suitcases were unstrapped, winter woolens
spewing wisps of camphor. Hats almost tossed
onto beds then . . . reconsidered.

One shoe drops on a wooden floor, while travelers below
look up, waiting in the lobby-wide pause in between.

Walking the Beach in the 21st Century

I know
there are no right angles in nature, yet
this driftwood stick I hold has one,
perhaps a stem of grapevine or hedge trained
square around a garden trellis.

I use
the stick to poke at slivers of sand dollars,
heart-shaped agates half-buried in sand
at the edge of the shoreline, encroaching
tide erasing my steps behind me.

I prod
a small carcass, crouch to
make out its original form from the
shape of decomposition. It's round as
a skipping stone—maybe a mollusk
of some kind, fist-sized lump of
membrane and muscle. Then

I notice
the lines running parallel like thin
red and black veins just beneath the
cracked, encrusted shell that turns out
to be a plastic case that even
salt water couldn't corrode and

I realize
this is the body of a mouse. Not a
drowned rodent, wet fur betraying
the truth of its slightness, but a
computer clicker thrown or washed into
the sea. A few steps away,

I find
half a keyboard—the left half, where
the A's and S's and E's reside. Someone in
a literal rage against the machine has taken it
over their knee or, grabbing one side, smashed
it against concrete repeatedly, the way waves
pummel rocks, thereby gaining some measure
of revenge for a deleted file or blank screen.

I stand
at the lip of a lagoon, the melding
of a local creek with the ocean, watch a
flock of gulls pick at a large fish. The head
is decayed and only the last half-yard of
spotted tail is intact. But enough remains to
identify it as a shark, its tough flesh yielding
to the twist and tug of beaks.

I see
a hook set in what's left of the shark's mouth,
attached monofilament kinked and writhing
in the onshore breeze. The midsection is slit,
spread neatly as if for an autopsy: glistening
schematic of organs and vessels visible, the
inspired design of its circuitry revealed.

I kneel.

The Half-Life of Memory

It's as toxic as any nuclear mountain,
though it's a mountain that comes to you.
It's not out there beside some wasted stretch
of Nevada 50 or among the radioactive rabbits
on the high plains of eastern Washington
where tumbleweeds choke the fences
and little rodent deaths foul the wells.

You are the soldier it was tested on,
the shadow vaporized onto the wall.
Take off your goggles, your white
hazmat suit, ignore the Geiger's chittering.
To look back is to risk becoming salt
like the linings of subconscious dumps
half a mile beneath southern New Mexico.

Memory's waning anticipates yours.
It decays before your bags are even packed,
was last seen traveling toward the vanishing point
of a half-lived life. A mirror with degraded silver;
you see through it without reflection.
It's spent fuel, seems safe and clean,
fools you into thinking exposure won't incinerate.

But even showers of alkaline regret
can't prevent contamination.
You don't have enough years to wait it out,
enough concrete to contain it.

Three Fates

I. Weaver

A white egret flies under a white bridge,
gray legs stretched out behind and for a moment
freeze-frames the morning fog and
the creep of tide up the banks,
the cruciform reflection of the egret,
the white arch of the footbridge
(which is water and which is sky
and which is warped by barely perceptible
ripples of something feeding beneath?),
the egret's flight defining architecture of light
and bridge, the passage of water to ocean and back,
the daylight moon setting behind leaf-barren trees,
the sun rising above a house that extrudes
piano concerto through curtains open to the canal
where sleeping sea ducks float, heads tucked,
necks so much stockier than the egret's,
which is like thick white cord threaded to
the yellow beak, sewing the air to the water,
the water to the bridge, the bridge to the bank,
through the loops of music, the fabric of fog,
the braided sticks and down of pouchy swallow nests
hung beneath the concrete arch
where now the white wings of the egret reemerge,
drawing all above and all below into
something tight and nearly seamless.

II. Allotter

This is what we are given:
years like floating leaf haiku,
candle boats upon the current,

the same current that erodes the banks
and makes them crumble in muddy chunks,

scooping larger and larger until
the bow of the river takes a sweeping turn

and we miss the flickers passing out of reach,
distracted by the jigging of red crawfish.

A full heart, then an empty home.
A full belly, then nothing left to devour.

The body betrays the mind.
The mind betrays the heart.

And memory betrays them all,
the river a lie of omission.

III. Not Turning Back

Memories are luminescent squid
risen, become visible on the surface.
Seasons are waves arriving
one after the other, each reaching further
up the beach. The squid, moon, and waves
collude with the undertow of the past,
pulling you steadily to depth.

And you've always wanted this time
to ponder how it is you came to be treading:
the choices and branchings,
the charities of coincidence;
bundles put down or picked up,
how far you were willing to carry them.
Your sister, your sister, your sister,
your mother trying to outshout the sea,
your father's silence disapproving
from the grave. Your wives . . .

Decisions made in shallows,
the courses changed, stayed, corrected,
sometimes rowing, sometimes
just giving in to the drift. The wind a lull,
the wind a friend pushing from behind,
and eventually even the wind against you.

The water is woven with squid,
faint blue glimmers under the swells
that stretch to the horizon, which is
the edge of a box that holds the whole arc
of bay, the whole of teeming sea,
and in its lid are tiny pinpricks where
light from somewhere else leaks through.

Blur

Out east on the desert freeway,
after the rain blowing in from the coast
had been blocked by the mountains doing their work,
the sky was fearless and the sun, half arisen now,
cast shadows of slow-whirling wind turbine blades
across all eight lanes, passing over each car
like the shadow of a hunting hawk.
A man in front of a prefab church
changed letters on the sidewalk marquee.
"God is waiting . . ." it began but I went by too fast
to see if He was waiting for me.

Jan Wesley

Jan Wesley is the author of *Only So Much* from What Books, her second full-length poetry book. Her first book is titled *Living in Freefall*, and she has two published chapbooks.

Her poems have appeared in *Askew, Blue Mountain Review, The Iowa Review, Rattle, Spillway, Beyond Words*, and anthologies, including *Angle of Reflection*, and she received a Pushcart nomination. She worked in post-production in the film business for many years, and after receiving an MFA at Vermont College, she taught writing at The University of Redlands and The Fashion Institute of Design and Merchandising, and co-hosted The Rose Cafe reading series in Venice. Currently, she facilitates writing workshops in Los Angeles.

Day One

The nurses whisper how the father was
asleep yet he stands by the worn-out mother

with the milky food, and arms of the nurse
lift me, relieve me from compression

in the birth canal, its endless quiet, and why
we struggle so, and so terribly soon is a mystery.

Mother—she must be—stares without a glance
away, her grin, her willowy hands strong

and what I yearn for as she smooths the matted
hair into a cap on my head. Burps of sudden delight

can't predict how we will flourish, how sickly
the moods will come to mangle the family one day.

A person's finger to the chin is a springboard
to kindness and they say this is memory shifting

and I never knew the mouth could work itself
and chew the air, the father's eyes sky blue,

my first lesson in color. In eighty years
the father will perish, the mother's agonies grown

like fescue flowing from the garden, a harsh
world quick to pity, to break her. These are voices

that were whispered to the mother's belly, the alto
being hers, the loud music of vocabulary his.

I see I will get more of his words, like *justice*
and *vigilance, history* and *art* and *remember,*

as they hand me over, tell me my name,
changing what I can see in the room. The shape

of a breast comes to my mouth, no longer being
fed alone in the dark, and feet wriggle with freedom

like the first chilly shiver from my mother's touch
as it rushes like water over the skin of my new face.

That Lingering Need for Ritual

Back then, as we say these days of *those* days the world was open, revolving, the body in masterful form when a stretch of tendons attached to solid bones could get me to another family holiday. Garden sprouts hid in single seeds and corners of the earth peeled back to reveal science like small animals studied in careful hands. Soon the century changed, and we lost sense of the risk of uncalculated danger the way a child might mangle fingers in a toy. We lose sight of forests and the land is laden with theft and short breath behind the throat, no end to strip-mined streets where someone's dinner lies tilted in the garbage. This holiday of thanks comes with excess food, frozen streams of cars loaded with ritual offerings, the leaves on trees turning red, yellow and dropping when they're through. I don't get soothed by turkey or lulled by tryptophan, the armor of football on tv unable to protect us anymore from family silence and squabble, and we collapse into drunkenness expecting to be forgiven once again. I ramble off somewhere between dessert and sleep to a steamy motel by the beach and a man lazes on the chilly sand. Like a habit we slide a card to enter a room, the smell of him leading me to our brief reunion. I know this kind of escape is cliché, but when my mother took her life, I couldn't find solace in family commiseration and reasoning, so I found men who expected nothing except flesh and lusty animal sounds, a frenzy of the body being hushed and calmed by whispers of a stranger. He and I lean in the doorway and the moon shapes itself into a half dome along the horizon, our hands resting on tapped-out stomachs, our heads fallen back to breathe in a hundred thousand stars a minute.

Taking Cover

I watch finches streak beyond
the glass, imagine life
without shame
without having done it all at a tilt.

Tomorrow rain might come
for good, the earth's strained
crops desperate and licking their lips
under abused terrain.

Hemispheres of the brain
are inundated with this life
contained in them

as if the mind is
a cupboard, a cavernous place
my mother would scavenge
for relief of forgotten
wine, for smells of dried lilac

and cooking sherry
disappearing more
quickly than the meals
she poured the spirit into. She would

stir and stir with her hands
fluttering like parakeets above
the stew as it bubbled over—

killing the flame
until my father got home, his
dread on fire as he found his wife
so changed from the love

he had felt in the morning. Home
in the afternoon I mastered duties
to hide liquor, set a table, put cutting
boards on the counter, yank

apart celery stalks
with my hand on her hand
to take the knife away before

my father's cautious head
nudged through the door
and like a match to gasoline
the words of blame invaded

the house and left
my ears shuttered against bellows
of the fight. With a flurry
of feet I let the screen door tremble
behind me, where empty sinuous

roads ran like rapids beneath
my flight and the boys
swooped in to make me

weightless beneath stabs of a sizzling
sun, its heat inked into us,
unfastened sneakers running
and running into the vistas
from only so much we could take.

Nothing Tied Down

After the arguments, my mother would change how she moved, hands limp at her sides, head lowered to the cross of her legs, neck swooped like a swan's. Swabs of evening sky swept through the woods along the house while I placed utensils on cloth mats of the dinner table, unclipped a field of laundry and tilted my ear toward my parent's fight. One night, mother planted me in the car, father dimming in the driveway, tools and boxed-up remnants of our lives lost behind the garage door as we sped off and bolted down the interstate to Maryland where her sister took us in. Perhaps we stayed overnight, perhaps it rained and in the glisten of morning sun I slept all the way back home.

Tonight, the mind fights sleep with flashes of fire in the canyon as I ache for mother's zeal of being uprooted and I wonder what to take if the fire leaps the ravine. Television in the room spits evacuation orders as I pack up mother's letters to me before she died. Newscasters hesitate in the following hours and so it seems we've been spared by wind direction, erasure of nature confined to unhoused acres of hillside grass. The smoke will linger for days, September's dried sticks scuttling across the road like the sound of fingernails dragged along a desk, maple leaves sending messages from my mother, reminders *not to argue with my father, to turn off the stove. Remember to be home soon.*

Great Escapes

After the first martini she is radiant, persevering man beside her delighted by a flourish of her hand as he goes on with his story of a dog run down in Beverly Hills, and he does go on, tidbits regarding the market, wizardry of masseurs, and soon the drone of him makes her love the ease of ordering another, mind skipping lightly to the edge of a fuzzy universe where she uncorks at the waist as he slips his hand between her hip and the bar stool she steps from like she's coming off a train. Sailing to the john, her black pump shoves the door open to green-tiled basin, its surface slick and gleaming like a mirror, and by morning a note says he carried her, she was light as air, and he leaves her two aspirin, a lost earring, his out-of-town number. When she wakes, I make her breakfast of tomato juice with vodka, study how pepper twirls but never mixes in, a sadness settled in her like a tiny hotel where the pain resides, where she wanders its halls and checks in on traveling lovers, on the dead, on our father screaming at us for something no one did. When I leave she flashes her toes to the sun, clicks the chaise down, one, two, three, reminds me to bury her in our hometown, in Renton, reminds me to dance on her grave the way we did when they buried Jimi Hendrix under a plaque no larger than an oversized Hershey bar, his grandmother next to him under identical plaque, dead at one hundred, sleeping with one eye open just a stride away, a stride away, simple vigilant stride away.

Inner Ear

I saw the whole piece immediately before my eyes and only needed to write it down, as though it were being dictated to me.

—Gustav Mahler referring to his symphony #8

My father made me listen to Mahler. I was ten and he was eternally in love with classical composers, especially the ones who wrote as if every concerto or symphony would be their last, might even save the world. An uncle in the Navy—electronics wizard married to my mother's sister and always silent about what he did—built my father a mono record player and speakers that today could blast hip-hop and Led Zeppelin like the best equipment designed to whirl us through space. When mother was out of the house shopping, perhaps finding liquor or selling her cameras to buy it—surreptitiously and with grief in her heart—my father would put on jazz or Mahler and crank up the volume until the whole neighborhood resounded like a concert hall. I loved how different he was from other parents—Eisenhower voters and war boosters even in the Vietnam years when 3000 Pennsylvania boys died with ears ringing from Howitzer fire and grenades. On occasion my father would play Rachmaninoff for herculean complexity and speed, remembrance of visceral passages of Concerto #2 when his own father took him to see Rachmaninoff play Rachmaninoff at Carnegie Hall. And sometimes I wish I'd been with my father before I was born—for the music—for Ella, Art Tatum, Gillespie and Monk. Tonight, I sit in a seat so high above the music center's stage I'm afraid I could pitch over the railing, but I don't. Instead, both movements of Mahler's 8th symphony overwhelm my body with 200 voices, concentric layers of strings, timpani, tubas and horns, crescendos so grand I boil over with what magnitude can do, with what *we* can do when we are guided by another person's hand, when we listen and surrender, when we love this life enough.

Elegy Two: Knowing

My mother is dying and I am the only one
who knows it. On days she is at peace
she brushes her hair fifty times and looks like
Ava Gardner, manages my eggs, my favorite
shirt, the timing of the bus. Days like that
she and I *own it*, roll it around in our hands
and then I imagine it's years later, people
cooing how much I look like her, how
pensive I've become with the omnivorous
eyes of a pelican. On days she starts drinking
misery sits with me at school and when
the bus dumps me home at four she
is weaving, smoking, a hole in her dress,
asleep on her side collapsed into shame
and suddenly I am running with impatient
boys, staring at a kid's chest measuring how
tall he is—the same time watching the house
where mother breathes like an anvil weighs
down her torso, the almost invisible tremors,
so I drive her to shop for liquor without any
smell until one afternoon she slips away.
The last time I run into her is in a dream
years after her death on a downtown street
where I live, her wavy hair lifted like a kite
and we talk with a strain that snaps muscle
from bone, questions like where have I been?
did I go to college? how's my father? and I
answer carefully as I did when she drank. She
asks what I do and I say *film* and her head tilts
in a gesture of interest, says she wants to see
one I made, and I tell her *yes*, don't want to be
pushy, her stance shying away as I tell her
to call me when she has time. Traffic moves
like a parade, population gutted by heat as she
turns to get on with her day and without
the touch she used to rub on me like a salve.

Separation is a dance and I step back from her
ghost, sudden transparency lost in a crowd
and when I wake at home in a sweat with
patterned clothes strewn across a chair, I see
she is not my mother now and I am not among
the dead, her shroud of secrets forever held
back from the living of why she had to leave.

Rough Trade

There is a poster of an ape on the wall, mouth wide,
holding a rock above his head twice the size of his hand

and in his other grip he mangles a strip of film
that flutters like a tattered flag. The movie is nailed

into place by numbers on a hard drive, now, the room

open past its bedtime. The man who keeps me late
has grey tincture to his face and likes to call out *honey*

babysweetheart, as he touches my weary shoulder
to signal he wants me to *cut*   the shot   *here*.

The machine heats to a hum and my fingers almost

blister on the knob in constant shuttle from stop to go.
Illusion subdues reason. I slide a fancy netted-seat chair

back from the screen and his mood is brooding, perhaps
unhappy with me, with my choices, and buttons

of his shirt have come undone. With him I keep the number
of studio security in my pocket, and critical to survival

and keeping my job, I lie to him, convince him my son

is coming home, that I must unlock the door to meet
and feed the kid a late-night meal. The man never

ever knows I don't have a son or if I did, he wouldn't care
as I exit the place through a land of innuendo and close in

the ape, the boss who doesn't look up, dangerous smoke
filling the room, the way special effects create disaster. He

lights a cigarette in the dark, takes a hit and I leave him
perhaps forever, as he sits by himself in his radioactive glow.

Lying on the Floor and Lying to Oneself Are Equal in Stature

*Age is something that doesn't matter,
unless you are a cheese.*

—Luis Buñuel

One day with birds at the window and pastries in the oven, a smear of grease grabs my rubber sole and pitches me into the sink and like a ball off a 9-iron the lean clink of head onto blemished linoleum forces my eyesight to sail into the distance. If I were a person with deliberation and calm, I might have learned to gaze at the steps I take, to recover quickly before I am prone on my own floor. I feel the cool of the surface like a child post-tantrum and ask if there are better ways to avoid the rabbit hole. Oh, fuck it, I think, let me take a minute to recover from shame of instability and the ability to save myself, some slip of breeze flitting through the window to soothe me. The body knows there is nowhere to go but up, so I push with a working woman's hands, a twist of torso, a heft in my knees to stand at five foot one and pat myself down, finding the bones have held themselves together.

My day goes on, and I make fifty more mistakes, achieve a few good deeds like pitching mail into recycle bins that teach us to use things more than once. My friend phones, says we should cruise the bars like days of sex without love and I tell her *yes*, time for a prison break and wishful thinking we are young in some low-lit club, the cloth of a man's shirt brushing my back as he reaches for another drink and turns too close to my face to ask if I want one, and I will say *yes*. I will dress in ambiguous clothes before my friend swings by and we will flirt, sip double-barreled specialty drinks, eat from a platter of diverse cheeses, accidentally bump a couple guys' thighs and lose a little balance against their table. We will remember the years they would ask us home, certain we will never hear those words again as we get into our valeted car with a little heat in the seats, observing the signs and weaving back into ourselves at that big bang of midnight.

Come On and Take It

. . . each time I tell myself I think I've had enough,
I'm gonna show you, baby, that a woman can be tough

—Janis Joplin

I always knew something was wrong with the movie business. Making movies is synonymous with being Someone, with knowing privilege and being protected from mundane dramas of real life. In this company town I can't stop seeing scenes from the business played back to me. To this day, I still throw myself into the clutch of the wrong men, drink too much, and nerves in my body fall asleep. As I slink about in corners of strip-searching situations, or I can't find my scarf and purse and keys, I still wait to be saved in the last ten minutes of the final reel. Bosses loved to flaunt language like *courage, academy award performance, brilliant decision, astonishing moment, great legs, come to poppa*, and just like that my mind roams like a flurry on a slide guitar. In movies, characters somehow manage shock and fear in situations we could never actually handle when a hooded person with a 10-inch knife stands over our beds while we sleep. Sometimes there is the bluster of an actress strutting into a room on the edge of a plunging hill where she flops on a sofa, kicks off red-soled Louboutin heels, shows dismay without wrinkling skin or hair and curses the latest man, saying dialogue like, *I shoulda' killed the bastard.* A producer used to tap my shoulder and tell me he wanted to linger on the actresses' pouty lips so that every woman in the audience wanted to be her. I'd spin the knob to leap further into the scripted plot of another bank job, and the she-thief might seduce the top-dog robber who appeared from somewhere unknown, perhaps from the balcony through an unlocked door. A weariness would come over me, and I wanted to weep from small inconsequential things like running out of cat food. Like a lightning strike, he liked to yell at me to *toughen up*, I'm *too nice*, and on weekends I believed him, avoided people who took gentle meanderings along the ocean and learned how to jump out of airplanes instead. It can be hard on the spine and shoulders but I was young and believed everything would heal. The producer could mangle the air with a throat clearing and without closure, might say, *I gotta meet a guy who knows a guy*, so *wrap it up*, and I'd hear choral music as if I were about to be sprung from the slammer. My stomach chattered for food as I shut the machine down when suddenly, with sweetness, he called his daughter, which like too many unremarkable things almost made me cry. He told her he knows a guy and she can have what they both want at the coveted college across town, as in no test scores, a starting position on the soccer team. There was pause for her voice, then producer laughed and answered, *piece of cake*, and I got hungrier, which made me forget if this was a movie or some version of real life, and whether I should stay in a wide shot or go into a close-up as she said, *I love you, daddy. Everybody does.*

History Repeats Itself, Repeats Itself

The whole world is watching . . .

—Demonstrators' chant, Democratic Convention, 1968

1.
On the porch, Maggie's daughter, the size of a Great Dane, in thrift-store snowsuit scrapes one leg past the other, opens the flaps of a television-sized carton, hands cold despite mittens attached by safety pins to each sleeve. The box is the size of her world, her mother inside pawing through mail and sales ads for offers she can't afford. Husband or dad, depending on who remembers him, is supposed to be alive in Iraq, Maggie and the girl finding solace in freezing weather with bone soup on a single-burner stove, in clothes Maggie makes from other clothes.

2.
Fire burns up the chimney, its ashes causing the soldier's wife to wheeze from scorched kindling of front-page news that repeats itself, repeats itself —the president a criminal and still no jail, no death by shame, not one rusty nail to seal his coffin.

3.
People surge into the streets, the too-young-to-fail saving trees, bodies close as nerve endings striking pavement of the boulevard to stop the Nazis, stop the guns, stop the chemicals flown onto food, stop the murder of black women's children killed by police. And killed by police. In history, mothers rage against wars and how it takes their sons and then the next ones.

4.
The young girl paws the inside of the box tipped over onto the porch. The house reshapes itself under eaves burdened with snow as Maggie rubs her hands, pulls her shoulders around her chest to create warmth, uncrates the girl, swoops her inside, kicks the door to close against the cold. Dinner is flimsy but there is wood, short pile of children's books, black and white tv, the girl sitting on the floor between her mother's legs, her hands around Maggie's tapered calves like prisoners' hands around the bars.

5.
On the news protesters stand face to face with police, messages scrawled on sides of cardboard boxes, fingers in fists, fingers spread in peace signs, police staring down another mother of a dead son, and just like parents who stand in the street waiting for their kids to hustle home after another stash of weapons sends perpetuity of people to unsuspected death—here we go—here we go again.

Bleed

*The blood moves through the body in a circle,
moving into the heart and then back out
of it on the other side.*

The List reminds me what to do, who to co-mingle with, and every day I add a different task, plan meals, shell out a bundle for excess and self-pleasure. Before noon I make it to the grocery, the warehouse where UPS takes things back, garden shop showing off succulents in the wrong season for peonies, dog trainer for Maxie's bites and yowls, a thousand dollars to the bank to pump up possibility I will be all right. My lover is not on my list any longer, circling through me without returning to the heart, sudden failings swept to the far side of the house where the dog snarls and flares his mouth. My hours for sleep in tossing-churning nights have faded with the stars and leave me weary as I stand at the window and see how rain has frozen and slabbed the mountains with snow. Purity and glisten bleed from the clouds strung along the sky, circling peaks above the valley, acres of shadows like an overflow of woefulness in this town where the real comes in one side and surreal flows out the other. This city suffers from *worst* bloated traffic, *best* deceptive hustle, and he wants my bare, shivering flesh, its chafing and reshaping of us as he drags his hands along my difficult bones. I have pleased too many people and scampered too hard, and still, I believe survival and justice are within reach. The morning bleeds into a sharp-edged day and I kick aside flung clothes to clear a path to the end of dishevelment and tell him this isn't enough, this re-routing of touch, our fist-sized hearts losing rhythm. I know I will bleed a few tears and the dog licking my face will save me from regret. I open the drapes onto the oddity of snow in a place where we are eternally doused in sunlight, its soundless devotion reliable in the way blood fills the wings of a bird before it takes off in unmistakable flight.

Love Fallen to the Ground

1.
It does zoom by when I think about it. Life, I mean. Birds in a storm. Whoosh, *hello, goodbye.* Everyone so afraid. Of death, I mean, of 200 species a day dying without a gravestone, clear-cut homes flattened to ash in blazes worse than...Worse than what? When memory spits like bees, I remember my small legs bent in a hunch over fur-topped holes in the yard where bunnies huddled. Before I'd reach inside, or as I did, my mother would say, *don't touch the babies or their mothers will leave them.* Another nature story. Often, we slink away from touch, but most days she corralled me with her hand cupped around my elbow to lead me on this path or another, out of the disappearing woods, to find gentlest ways to grow me. When we tell a story, we often start with, *feels like yesterday . . .* then action and consequence, understandable doubt.

2.
Is memory like life flashing before my eyes as they say it does: flammable hills in a drought, limping creatures in dying grass, light, light, damn light along his back in flapping shirt through the field of vines, death of horses on a racetrack buckling to the dirt, my husband weaving on a ship deck before we leave the port, his breath snaked around my hair, the snake on our picnic rock, kissing in stairwells, kissing in public before we reached the top floor?

3.
The body itches to shed itself and my vision wafts through the room where our years together chafe like wind chimes. This town is getting swept back to its second layer, sometimes by fire, sometimes by the days we knew so much—abundant food dropped from trees, protection of mountain tops cleaned like feathers from fowl, disappearance of animals taken for granted the way a lizard loses a tail, jungles lose cover to machetes. The night brings on smell of gasoline, smack of a car door, voice insistent with *hello, hello, anybody there?* I walk out into the sigh of exodus taking over the city, warm air against the skin, soft scents mumbling through windows, a hand fallen across my face so that finally I can sleep.

Brenda Yates

Brenda Yates is from nowhere. After growing up on military bases, she settled first in Boston and then Los Angeles. She is the author of *Bodily Knowledge* (Tebot Bach) with poems, reviews, interviews, flash fiction and hybrids in publications based in Australia, Canada, China, England, India, Ireland, Israel, Japan, the Netherlands, Portugal and the US, including *Adelaide; Aji; Anesthesiology: Journal of the ASA; Antigonish Review; Brush Talks; Catamaran; Chaparral; Chatauqua; erbacce; MacGuffin; Mississippi Review; Pratik; Seaside Gothic; Shanghai Literary Review; Surreal Poetics; Wallace Stevens Journal*. Notably, she was a Kyoto, Letheon, Princemere, Sundress, Apple In The Dark, Wolverine and Robinson Jeffers Tor House finalist as well as a Pushcart and Best-of-the-Net nominee. Awards include the Patricia Bibby and Beyond Baroque Literary Arts Center Poetry Prize.

Alphabet-flower ABC's

Anemones belie
carnivorous design,
effecting flowery genus,
hiding in jaded knotty
languor. Marks never
observe predators' quick
reach. Sudden tentacle,
until very woozy,
xerotic, yes, zombie.

Brevity

as when   cherry blossoms   take your breath: festival of bursting into bloom   petals   everywhere   dizzied eyes   like drunken doves   in faintly fragrant   pink-

swirled air   a fragile few days   anticipated   seasonal   drift   even the busy participate in   that any of us

might grasp   mourn   and   remember   one of many arts celebrating that which passes—

beauty   because   it's   fleeting   those very same reasons   ancient people   could call their   gods

unlucky.   Immortals   cry   grieve   get jealous   or bored   like   any   human   but they   can never

behold   majestic fluorescent butterfly   bird of paradise   flower tree canyon   nor even   turquoise sea   and feel

awe. That   profound   sense   available only   to ungods,   ones   who will leave these things,   leave   blessed

with a mortal's   reverence   for life   for breath   that can take in such wonders   before   our   ungodly end.

Dream Song Philtre

Sometimes, after a long absence
even the long-married lie
together like strangers

stranded in an almost familiar place
where not quite understood
consonants keep tilting away

into unfamiliar language.
Sometimes even the long-married
must become more patient,

re-translate, re-interpret vowels
of hesitant mouth, tentative hand
until suddenly the old intimacies

remember desire's secret tongue of long,
sweet sex intimate, now, and effortless.
Sometimes then, long-married

bodies, after stuttering into sleep,
curve into long slumbers of silk yeses,
yeses loud enough to waken dreams,

which, re-acquainting themselves,
leave their rooms of waxy light,
and press together, talking in the low

voices of lovers, long-time lovers
who speak softly their private
dialect of hibiscus and hyacinth.

Cauldron of Blue Light

Crater Lake: water like scattered stars
and so deep its stillness
touches shore unmoved. A pure blue

no stream flows into, made of rain and
snow melt, touched only
by immaculate air. Tranquil, heavenly?

No, bluer—more sacred than the Mother
of God's garment when
she held the Child in her lap, the one

that painters invented a new color for.
Bluer than angel voices,
than all her head-coverings and gowns.

Than the royal sapphires, tanzanite
and blue diamonds exciting
ancient frequencies. Than visible energy

or shivering glaciers about to calve. Bluer
than the "O" to which
Rimbaud promised: *Someday, I will*

open your silent pregnancies. Divine
blue. Dream blue,
dormant eye blue. Azure more saturated

than lapis lazuli and without the veins,
gold or not.
Dawn's unbroken day still wrapped

in indigo. Blue containing
all blue.
No use comparing. Fact is: caldera

forged by fire, filled with sleet,
ice, blizzard,
thunderstorm, and, still, drinking

furies blown from the ocean's
immense wrath,
its clarion wind a thought repeating itself.

And so we are here again: bluer than
an imperial affliction
that steals us from our lives,

like arguments of time that change
reality—blue
memories of glacier, volcano collapse,

bowls of sky. Blue as the spell you
fall under
when looking into its depths

and cannot tell where it ends or that
anything else begins.
As when *you are moved*, Dante says,

by a light that is formed in heaven—
having known,
having felt perhaps, the way color

and light take possession of us.
The way they
change energy. As in our blue-green

origins or those organs before eyes,
detecting light
and wild with it, surviving because of it.

Not a frivolous surface intensity,
but penetrating
through skin into flesh of living beings.

Dangerous droplets, blue as love, green
as paradise,
singing the world to our innermost

selves, attracting, igniting future,
igniting potential.
Who hasn't wondered at the intoxication

of a wilderness, dappled or not,
in our make-up?
Or thought about the necessary

complications of its whys. A virus,
entering our cells,
replicates itself from within, until

it's as if these cells were that self
all along, helpless
as flowers bending toward light.

Toward colors contagious as words
that once doled out
unfold like origami reversing itself.

Komorebi, Japanese call it,
the light that
filters through the leaves of trees,

definition that carries ghost
understandings
of an ancient life drawing us

out of ourselves. Drawn into and
then away,
out into the cerulean world,

no matter where on earth
we've come
to live and breathe:

exhaled from the seasons of ourselves.

Even Without the Minotaur,

it's that old story of intrigue and uncontrolled lust, shame and secrets, of subterranean passages undermining society's airy castles. No matter how well-built. Because any fortress is as vulnerable as a beautiful mind and can come to be riddled with beasts creating their own combinations of fear, violence, death. Still the case and even way back then, fame meant fathers (there were few famous mothers) built prisons for themselves—and for their children—whether or not that's what they set out to do. Already complications were evident in those labyrinthine etymologies. The word "clue," for instance, means: ball of yarn, agglomeration of things, or thread of life spun by the Fates. Enter Icarus. Like any boy growing up in his father's shadow, he wanted to escape constraints. Hubris? Or just reckless, on a wing and a prayer. Overly ambitious or giddy with freedom? A primal concordance, perhaps. Or all those things: yet another embodied contradiction with a dreadful need to return to his mother's waters. Whatever you call it, he fell. As humans do.

"Death is Nothing"

I smudge that epitaph. What you had carved on your headstone:
clear intentions we didn't want to believe. But no mosaic of lock-
up, talk, meds, understanding, nor even love could change what

you considered ongoing choice. Undertow. Under-world current.
Subterranean river. I know you'd say nothing came for them just
the same; nothing carried their bodies to graves now grown over

with the cemetery grass you once called great green seas where,
accepted or not, all of us go down like storm-shocked boats; we
drown no matter the lanterns or hearts still lit. *Is everything . . . is*

there something . . . anything . . . no it's nothing . . . nothing . . . filling
spaces between your fingers as you played piano, washing over
words you sang or the long, low, funny notes you liked to hold,

flooding memories of nothing's foreshadows as they cut into
your bones. Should I have known you bled more than the rest
of us? That absent marrow blood, bones fill with sloughs

of nothing? Did your nothing burst into silence? Did it empty
as when a chorus of crickets suddenly stops? Still, you don't
answer. So let me tell you again. I don't know if anyone any-

where can ever know anything beyond whatever sorrows
inhabit us (voiceless or not) except that they will live as long
as we refuse nothing.

Safe

Shut in darkness, you have done with this: the all too soon, the slow, the fast, the numb procession of years. You have done with spring, with its fire burning brightly like some spiteful god who brings no peace. You are done as well with every fall, turning, and returning, to toll again in the shocked bell of your body. And also, bereft of politics, patriotism and the polysyllabic rhetoric of fear, you are done with conflict. Done now with any promises or words, broken and floating skyward. And free from the myriad mouthless dead whose dreams still wander like orphans. No need for warnings, abstractions, or euphemisms for die. No need to remember. Done too are once more, somewhere, anywhere, all those certainties of always, never, or maybe someday. Yes, you are finally done with hurting or wanting or even believing, and with wishes for untime, unspring, unkill, unwar.

Go in Abstraction by Sevens with Adverbs

You are meant to get lost here
        among words in a country
                of words—diaphanous words

holding a plea against some
        wretched, hard reality,
                against precision's pinned-down

rage minutely dissecting
        one more hapless pain, against
                edgy acid ironies

lying uneasily on
        open satin-lined caskets—
                imprecise words (joy/hope/love)

suspending death, that lifeblood
        of being alive. Words that
                see into the life of things,

brook the way one of childhood's
        long summer days lets go its
                miracles: steady but some-

how faintly glimmering like
        imaginary birds that
                might be souls, spirits or tricks

of light. You, me, all of us
        vulnerable as any
                naked thing born of burned-out

stars (or more correctly: of
        resurrected celestial
                energy) slowly rowing

    our nameless selves as if we
           were ghostly sculls noisily
                    slapping our inexpert oars

    out of a fog bank into
           the near clarity of in-
                    definable star-thick nights.

Seventeen Syllables Searching for Branches

It had come to pass
but spring stayed bare, a stillborn
veiled in snow and ice

while spirits, uncalled,
stood alone above the world,
struck dumb with no flesh.

Blossoms too were lost—
without form—couldn't entice
their lovers, the bees.

And bees live for love.
Their loud glad hums fell silent:
"Nothing matters now"

buzzed from hive to hive.
Then, locking themselves in their
cells they pined and swore

never to come out.
"What's the use?" But once again
though slumbering late,

nature stirred and spoke,
incited idiocies,
pricking hearts, bathing

vines and roots with sweet
rains, rioting the genius
of a honeyed world.

Interlude: Kyoto

Windows flung open, wide night brings itself indoors. But
never enough for me: no melancholy wannabe lotus-eater
long endures bitter onslaughts chilling down to my smallest
bones, bones which even now, despite spring, remember
and hunger after sun-baked warmth.

*

Rainy season days, cloudbursts, thundering restless nights
until wind turns, and dawn, breaking bright, fructifies
promises, ones that rise in the dark like colorless dreams
while feverish green ideas sleep furiously.

*

Overhanging heat, unruly July, ever-more lush August,
brings energy-sapping days, and nights too hot to sleep.
Our languished spirits— complaints voiced—bed down
for fitful slumber on not quite cool balconies.

*

Then another fall's fiercely vivid death: autumn leaves on
stoic ground and chilly air just right for a wandering walk's
long meditation. Or to watch robed monks chase American
children out of the temple after finding they'd climbed
behind Buddha to see what he looked like there.

*

Opening the door, I leave home. Winter's crisp breath
excites my bare face. You can laugh because you know
what's coming but hope's inexhaustible (although this year
might be almost identical): piled up, grotty snow, rutted,
ice-glazed roads, frozen eyelashes, burning lungs/cheeks/
ears/nose; fingertips, toes too cold to move, part of winter's
aged harvest of bones when no happiness need apply, only
waiting to fling this aside.

Nightmares

No lullaby's sweet good night
and gone is the innocent sleep

in the rocking skulls of children
still dreaming of the fairy tale

woes or the even somewhat grim,
though exceedingly just,

fabled comeuppance
accorded each and every

man, woman or child, all
those naughty fools, the unkind

or selfish, the haughty ones
too, no matter how rich,

nor if a prince or princess—
until now's ill-fated, sour orange

hella days, extending oh, no, no
into long nights that go on and on

after unbelieving eyes try to close.

Mariano Zaro

Mariano Zaro is the author of six books of poetry, most recently *Decoding Sparrows* (What Books Press, Los Angeles) and *Padre Tierra* (Olifante, Zaragoza, Spain). His poems and short stories have been published in anthologies and literary journals in Spain, Mexico and the United States. His translations include B*uda en llamas* by Tony Barnstone and *Cómo escribir una canción de amor* by Sholeh Wolpé. He is a professor of Spanish at Río Hondo Community College (Whittier, California).www.marianozaro.com

After the Diagnosis

The diagnosis was not precise.
It was not a name, an acronym,
a statement. For him, it was a noise.

Time will tell.
Maybe some of the tests
should be repeated. This is
a diagnosis by exclusion.
A spinal tap, lumbar puncture,
has been helpful, not always,
in similar cases.
But it's painful, you know.
And it wouldn't change
the treatment. Perhaps you are
in the very early stages
of something. And you already
have been referred
to behavioral health services.
We have support groups,
counseling, we are not going
anywhere. We have checked
all the boxes, haven't we?

That's when the patient left.
Then, he took a train, and another.

He thought that moving
would move the symptoms away.
That the distance would create
a space, like a valley or a meadow
between the body and its pain.

They have seen him helping the homeless,
cleaning their wounds with gauze and ointment.
They have seen him hitting a dog
with a wooden stick.

They have seen him in museums,
standing in front of paintings,
without blinking, for a long time,
as if beauty could cure anything.

They have seen him kneeling
before altars, burning fires
on an empty beach, at night,
waiting for the worries to dissolve.

He only wants to forget the symptoms,
without trying. Like when you change
trains and you leave behind your lunch box
with a half-eaten sandwich, or a book
you are reading, the ticket tucked between
two pages, or an old umbrella.

But he cannot forget the body
because the body doesn't forget you.

The body follows you wherever you go,
and sleeps with you every night,
like a lover who cannot breathe without
your lungs and, without your eyes
cannot wake up the next morning.

Enzymes

They are sitting at a table next to mine
in a small restaurant in Madrid,
near Atocha Station.
Father and daughter, I assume.

        Saliva contains enzymes that help catalyze
        chemical reactions in the body.

She is eight, maybe ten,
wears a summer dress—
white cotton with
small printed lemons.

        The major enzymes in saliva are salivary amylase,
        salivary kallikrein and lingual lipase.

I order a salad, mineral water—
something simple,
I don't like eating alone.
They order veal with mashed potatoes.

        Salivary amylase breaks down starches
        into smaller, simpler sugars.

When she drinks, the girl
lifts her glass with both hands.
The father is young, tells the waiter
to bring a spoon, an extra napkin.

        Salivary kallikrein increases
        vasodilation and capillary permeability.

The girl has short hair,
wears glasses fastened
to the back of her head
with a wide elastic band.

>Lingual lipase breaks down triglycerides
>into fatty acids and glycerides.

The father picks up
a small piece of veal with his fingers,
chews it slightly with his front teeth,
makes a paste
and puts it in his daughter's mouth.

>Another enzyme is acid phosphatase,
>which frees up phosphoryl groups from other molecules.

The girl smiles—gums swollen,
starts chewing, swallows,
looks at her father, grabs the spoon,
clenches her fist—the spoon
rattles against the plate.
She starts eating the mashed potatoes.
The father rests both hands on the table.

>Saliva also contains lysozymes that kill bacteria,
>viruses and other foreign agents in the body.

The restaurant looks brighter now,
even the street traffic is gentler.
I feel less alone.
I may order a glass of wine after all
to celebrate her victory.

Vocative

In the second declension in Latin
masculine nouns change in the vocative form.

The ending -us of the nominative
changes to -e in the vocative.

That's why the poet Catullus,
when talking to himself
in his poem number 8,
does not say "Catullus" but "Catulle":
"Miser Catulle, desinas ineptire"
(Wretched Catullus, stop being a fool)

Nouns ending in -ius change to -i.

When Catullus writes to Iuventius
in his poem number 48,
he does not say Iuventius, but Iuventi.
"Mellitos oculos tuos, Iuventi,
siquis me sinat usque basiare,
usque ad milia basiem trecenta,
nec umquam uidear satur futurus"
(Iuventius, If I could kiss
your honeyed eyes, I would kiss them
three hundred thousand times
and never be sated)

Vocative case is used
to address somebody directly.

My mother wakes up screaming
in the middle of the night.
She sits on her bed
and repeats her own name
as if trying to escape a trap.
Neck tense, face flushed,

she repeats her name
until she is exhausted, out of breath.
It's a dream, Mother, I say.
One of your bad dreams.

Her dementia makes her believe
that she is leaving the room.
Call her, she says. *Call her.*
She has to come back.

And I call her, I call you, Mother,
and I cover your shoulders
with your bathrobe.

I call you by your name intact
as it was in your baptism
ninety-four years ago.
I call you by your name dressed
in white for your first communion.

I call you by your name blushing
the day you met Father at age fourteen.
I call you by your name stained
with ashes when you lost your child.

I call you by your name ever changing
in all declensions: nominative, vocative,
accusative, genitive, dative, and ablative.

I call you by your name and all the names.
I call you by no name at all,
and kiss the top of your head
that smells like sweat.

The Weight of Sound

— Sir, you know how this works; just delete the last syllable of your words.

— Para seguir adelante.

— Yes, to move on you have to be lighter.

— Tan solo una sílaba.

— Only one, yes.

— La última sílaba.

— The last syllable, that's right.

— Por ejemplo . . .

— For example, *camino* becomes *cami*, *libertad* becomes *liber*, *amatista*, *amatis*.

— Nadie me entenderá.

— They will understand. Millions of people are already done with the upgrade.

— Me da miedo el cambio, tanta pérdida.

— Change may be scary. But you don't lose much. Few sounds here and there.

— Me da tristeza.

— It's not as sad as you think. You are shedding weight, remember.

— Algunas palabras tienen solo una sílaba.

— Of course, some words only have one syllable. I am aware of that.

—

—

— ¿Puedo decirlas por última vez?

— Yes, you can. Some of them. You can say them one last time before crossing.

— Adiós *mar, sal, sol, luz, bien, mal, más, pez, pan, sí, ser, paz, tú, voz, no*.

Mariano Zaro

On a Silver Platter

The world has become heavy, I tell my doctor.
A door's handle, a page in a book,
an empty glass.

I want you to see this, she says.
She points at the black-and-white image
on her computer screen.

She wears a wedding band, but I don't want to know
anything about her. I don't want her to have a husband,
children, parents, siblings.

This is your spine, she says. *From C-1 to L-5. Do you see these spots?*
Yes, I say. *What are they?*
Sadness, she says.

Are you sure? I ask.
It's a clear case, she says. *The location,*
the shape, the density.

Same patients present transparent sadness. We call it
Type Zero. Very difficult to diagnose, even using a dye for contrast.
Yours, however, is translucent. Type 1.

And it's shaped like pellets. You see? Very common in Type 1.
Type 2, the opaque sadness, is shaped like filaments that run
alongside the muscle fibers.

Type 1 stays close to the spine. May cause weakness,
trembling, paresthesia, night sweats,
sexual dysfunction.

There is also Type 3. It's web-shaped, settles around the neck.
Patients describe it as having a bridle around the throat.
Produces speech impediments, sometimes muteness.

The last identified sadness is called Inner Type, she says.
It generates in the amygdala. It looks like a rain
of electrical spores that can reach any part of the body.

Does the Type 1 explain all my symptoms? I ask.
We can't be sure, she says. *We are still in the early stages
of research. But sadness explains many things.*

What should I do? I ask.
*Some patients try to rest more and calm down.
But sometimes they fall into hypersomnia*, she says.

Balance is everything, she adds.
*Some patients cry. Some play sports for the
dopamine release. Some listen to music. Bach, most of all.*

I don't like sports, I say. *But I like Bach.
What do you do with your own sadness*, I ask.
I just keep plowing, she says.

Will I improve? I ask.
You will, she says. *But there is no cure for sadness.
It stays with you, always.*

What about the future sadness? I ask.
*We will cross that bridge when we get there.
Do you pray, meditate?* she asks.

Not really, I say.
How can the body function with all this sadness? I ask.
Nobody knows, she says.

*But some scientists theorize that the body wouldn't
be able to function without sadness.
Just a hypothesis.*

*Do you think we could survive
a lifelong load of sadness delivered in a single day?* I ask.
She plays with her wedding band.

Imagine your sadness, all at once, on a silver platter, I say.
All at once, she says, *on a silver platter,
like the head of John, the Baptist.*

At the Studio

my dance teacher tells
                me
my dance teacher gives
                me
a stone

                heavy
                dense
                warm

in my left hand
my dance teacher tells
                me
to hold

                smooth
                bigger than a big fist
                bigger than a big heart

tells me to dance

                a stone

the first step
to dance

                now
                and one, two, three, four

and I dance

                lopsided
                tilted
                slanted
                askew

the first step
I dance

                embarrassment

my dance teacher tells
                me
to dance

                happy embarrassment

                we all carry stones, you know

my dance teacher tells
                me

                just look around

Brother

Who is this boy? I ask my mother.
I am pointing
to a black-and-white picture
framed on a bookshelf.
He is your brother, she says.

The toddler is standing
next to a stroller,
wears a small hat.
It's a summer day.

This is not the first time
I have seen the picture.
This is the first time
we talk about it.
I am six years old.

Where is he now? I ask.
He is dead, my mother says.

What happens when you die? I ask.
Where do you go?

Nobody knows, she says.
Everything is the same.
Everything is not the same.

How did he die? I ask.
Fever, dehydration, she says.
What is dehydration? I ask.
He died of thirst, she says.

He was born April twenty-seventh,
nineteen sixty.
He died July eighteenth,
nineteen sixty-one.
It was a Tuesday.

I was born April fifteenth, I say.
Yes, April fifteenth nineteen sixty-three.
It was a Monday, she says.

All my children came to me.
All of them. All but you,
my mother says. *I looked for you.*
I had to look for you.
Because I was old, they said.

Where was I? I ask.
You were inside your father, she says.

Did my brother have toys? I ask.
Yes, she says. *But I told your aunts*
to take everything away.
His toys, his shoes,
all his clothing.
You shared the same crib, though.
But not the clothing.
I couldn't do that to you.

Was he better than I was, Mother? I ask.

She touches my hair.
He was strong, she says.
He brought you here.

Mouth to Mouth

KING CLAUDIUS: Now, Hamlet, where's Polonius?
HAMLET: At supper.
KING CLAUDIUS: At supper! where?
HAMLET: Not where he eats, but where he is eaten:
a certain convocation of politic worms are e'en at him.

—*Hamlet*, Act 4, Scene 3

We bury our dog at the end of the back patio.
My father and I. Next to the wooden fence.

The dog weighs 32 pounds, maybe 30 now.
He lost some weight since he was sick.

When we dig in the ground
we hit the roots of the neighbor's cherry tree.

>   Roots explore the soil, seeking out
>   water and mineral nutrients.

The shovel makes a hard noise
like metal against metal.

It's cold on this quiet October morning.
I wrap the body with a white towel.

I make sure the towel has no stains,
and fully covers his mouth and eyes.

>   Once mineral nutrients are dissolved in soil water,
>   they move into root cells by osmosis.

We mark the grave with a cross made
of small stones—three horizonal, four vertical.

My father goes to work.

I stay home until it's time to go to school.

A crow lands next to the grave,
starts pecking the freshly turned soil.

I wonder if the grave
is deep enough.

> Osmosis is the movement of water molecules
> to a solution of lower concentration.

The rain will scatter the cross stones.
It rains a lot in winter.

Come summer, the neighbor
will bring us his first cherries.

> Osmosis is possible because of the
> cells' partially permeable membrane.

We will eat the cherries—
the sweet and tart flesh.

I keep each pit in my mouth
until it's totally smooth.

Every fruit has its own soul,
my father says.

I will be somebody's food one day—
we become the ones who have eaten us.

Acknowledgments

Marjorie Becker
  "Piano Keys of Being." 2019 Finalist, Joy Harjo Prize, *Cutthroat Journal for the Arts*
  "Shad, Malomars." *Crosswinds Poetry Journal*, 2, 2023
  "Pie Filling." *"Crosswinds Poetry Journal*, 2, 2023
  "The Stash of Jewels." *Verdad*, Fall 2022, *Vol. 33*
  "Replete with Seers." *Interliq: California Poets, V*, September 2022
  "Golden Feather." *Interliq: California Poets, V*, September 2022

Jeanette Clough
  "Unknown." *Flourish* (Tebot Bach Press, 2017).
  "Imagining The Desert Trumpet." *Levure Litteraire #10*, 2014.
  "Silver Reef." *Beyond The Lyric Moment* (Tebot Bach Press, 2014).
  "Insects in the Desert." *Colorado Review 47.1*, Spring 2020, as "Desert Sonnet."
  "Moth." *The Inflectionist Review No. 3*, 2014; as "Un-Moth."
  "The Jasmine Corridor." *Spillway 26*, 2018.
  "Heist." *Flourish* (Tebot Bach Press, 2017).
  "Evocation (Streets)." *Bellevue Literary Review Issue 39*, Fall/Winter 2020.
  "Ardor." *Wisconsin Review Vol. 50, Issue 2*, Summer 2017.
  "Incognito." *Nimrod International Journal Vol. 60, #2*, Spring/Summer 2017.
  "Pillars of Light." *Pratik: The Ghosts Of Paradise—Special Los Angeles Double Issue—Vol. XVII, #2-3*, 2021.
  "A Story About Pianos." *Ibid*.
  "The Wonderfully Clear Transition." *Colorado Review 44.1*, Spring 2017.

Dina Hardy
  "Annotated Passengers (Song)." *The Canary*, 7.
  "Annotated Passengers (Superstition)." *The Canary*, 7.
  "Annotated Passengers (Sadness)." *Black Warrior Review*, 49.2.
  "Annotated Passengers (You)." *Black Warrior Review*, 49.2.

Paul Lieber
  "Hollows." *Parhelion Literary Magazine*, 2022; collected in *Slow Return* (What Books Press, 2024).

"Then it Became a Szechuan Café." *Interlitq*, 2023; collected in *Slow Return* (2024)

"A Request." *North Dakota Quarterly*, 2022; collected in *Slow Return* (What Books Press, 2024).

"Nonjudgmental." *Valley Voices*, 2021; collected in *Slow Return* (What Books Press, 2024).

"Empty." *North Dakota Quarterly*, 2022; collected in *Slow Return* (What Books Press, 2024).

"Breeze." *Interlitq*, 2023; collected in *Slow Return* (What Books Press, 2024).

"Slow Return." *Ghost City Review*, 2021; collected in *Slow Return* (What Books Press, 2024).

Sarah Maclay

"A Breathing Lake." *MORIA Online, Furious Pure* (reprint); collected in *Nightfall Marginalia* (What Books Press, 2024).

"A Mirror of Leaves." *Hotel Amerika*; collected in *Nightfall Marginalia* (What Books Press, 2024.)

"Real State." *Pratik—The Ghosts of Los Angeles, Special Los Angeles Double Issue*; collected in *Nightfall Marginalia* (What Books Press, 2024).

"After Vuillard." *Tupelo Quarterly*; collected in *Nightfall Marginalia* (What Books Press, 2024).

"It Is Not a Bridge." *Air/Light*; collected in *Nightfall Marginalia* (What Books Press, 2024).

"Rehearsal for Ending." *Manoa—Republic of Apples, Democracy of Oranges*; collected in Nightfall Marginalia (What Books Press, 2024).

"Hunger." *Air/Light*; collected in *Nightfall Marginalia* (What Books Press, 2024).

"Before Us." *FIELD*; collected in *Nightfall Marginalia* (What Books Press, 2024).

Holaday Mason

"So, What if the Chimes are Silent." *Spillway*, 2021; collected in *As if Scattered* (Giant Claw Press, 2024).

"And Both of Us Saw Tiny Spears of Violet." *As if Scattered* (Giant Claw Press, 2024).

"Lizards Are Always Dreaming." *As if Scattered* (Giant Claw Press, 2024).

"Shrine." *Towards the Forest* (New Rivers Press, 2007).

"Fire." *The Journal of Feminist Studies in Religion*, 2016; collected in *The Weaver's Body* (Tebot Bach, 2019).

"Menopause." *TQ14*; collected in *The Weaver's Body* (Tebot Bach, 2019).

"Prism." *Wide Awake: Poets of Los Angeles & Beyond*, 2015; collected in *The Weaver's Body* (Tebot Bach, 2019).

"The Edge of the World." *Poetry International*; collected in *The Weaver's Body* (Tebot Bach, 2019).

"Highway 99." *Pool*; collected in *Dissolve* (New Rivers, 2011).

"Towards the Forest." *Miranda Literary Review*; collected in *Towards the Forest* (New Rivers, 2007).

"From the Mountains to the Prairies to the Oceans, White with Foam." *Hotel Amerika, Vol. 18*.

Jim Natal

"Reading Lao Tzu, Sun Mountain, Santa Fe." *Transformation*.

"Sweet Home Chicago." *Interlitq V*, September 2022.

"The Sense of Touch." *In the Bee Trees* (Archer Books, 2000).

"Rain in L.A.: Thursday morning." *Runes*; collected in *Memory and Rain* (Red Hen Press, 2009).

"Moses." *The Café Review*; collected in *Talking Back to the Rocks* (Archer Books, 2003).

"Saguaro Motel." *Talking Back to the Rocks* (Archer Books, 2003).

"Tree of Life Hotel." *Talking Back to the Rocks* (Archer Books, 2003).

"Walking the Beach in the 21st Century." *Yalobusha Review*; collected in *Talking Back to the Rocks* (Archer Books, 2003).

"The Half-Life of Memory." *Memory and Rain* (Red Hen Press, 2009).

"Three Fates." *SOLO Café*; collected in *Memory and Rain* (Red Hen Press, 2009).

"Blur." *Askew*; collected in *Memory and Rain* (Red Hen Press, 2009).

Jan Wesley

"Day One." *Psychological Perspectives, Vol. 61, Issue2*, Summer 2018.

"that lingering need for ritual." *Spillway, #29*, 2021.

"Great Escapes." *Askew Magazine, #19*.

"Inner Ear." *Blue Mountain Review*, Spring 2020.

"Elegy Two: Knowing." *Sheila-Na-Gig Magazine, Vol. 5.1*, Fall 2020.

"Rough Trade." *Psychological Perspectives, Vol. 61, Issue 2*, Summer 2018.

"Lying on the Floor and Lying to Oneself Are Equal in Stature." *Spillway, #28*, 2020.

Brenda Yates
"Animal-flower ABC's." *DASH Literary Journal 8*, Spring, 2015; reprinted in *1001 Nights: Twenty Years of Redondo Poets at Coffee Cartel* (Redondo Poets, 2018).
"Brevity." *California Quarterly, Volume 45, Number 1* (California State Poetry Society).
"Dream Song Philtre." *Unmasked: Women Write About Sex and Intimacy After Fifty* (Weeping Willow Books, 2017).
"Cauldron of Blue Light." *Presence: A Journal of Catholic Poetry, Volume 5* (Caldwell University, Spring 2022).
"Even without the Minotaur." *Water On Water: Painted Poetry & Painterly Poetics—Ekphrastic Notions—Icarus Variations* (Joost de Jonge Books, Volume 3, 2020).
"Death is Nothing." *Essential: An Anthology* (Underground Writers Association, Portland, Maine September 2020).
"Safe." *Vine Leaves Literary Journal* (Vine Leaves Press, Jessica Bell Pub, Melbourne, Australia 2017).
"Go in Abstraction by Sevens with Adverbs." *Bending Genres Issue 10* (2019); reprinted in *The Compassion Anthology*, Spring 2020.
"Seventeen Syllables Searching For Branches." *Crosswinds Poetry Journal, Volume VII*, October 2021.
"Interlude: Kyoto." *Structures of Kyoto: Writers in Kyoto Anthology 4*, 2020 Writers in Kyoto Poetry Contest Third Place Winner.
"Nightmares." *Such An Ugly Time Anthology* (Rat's Ass Review, Winter 2017).

Mariano Zaro
"Vocative." *She Who Should Be Attention To: A Tribute to Suzanne Lummis.* Editors: Susan Hayden, Hanna Pachman and Jeremy Ra. Library Girl, (Ruskin Group Theater, Santa Monica, CA, 2022).
"On a Silver Platter." *Interlitq*, "Californian Poets, Part 4."
"At the Studio." *Beat Not Beat, An Anthology of California Poets* (Moon Tide Press, 2022).
"Brother." *Patterson Literary Review*, 2022.

Also Available from Moon Tide Press

Suffer for This: Sex, Drugs, Marriage, & Rock 'N' Roll, Victor D. Infante (2024)
What Blooms in the Dark, Emily J. Mundy (2024)
Fable, Bryn Wickerd (2024)
Diamond Bars 2, David A. Romero (2024)
Safe Handling, Rebecca Evans (2024)
More Jerkumstances: New & Selected Poems, Barbara Eknoian (2024)
Dissection Day, Ally McGregor (2023)
He's a Color Until He's Not, Christian Hanz Lozada (2023)
The Language of Fractions, Nicelle Davis (2023)
Paradise Anonymous, Oriana Ivy (2023)
Now You Are a Missing Person, Susan Hayden (2023)
Maze Mouth, Brian Sonia-Wallace (2023)
Tangled by Blood, Rebecca Evans (2023)
Another Way of Loving Death, Jeremy Ra (2023)
Kissing the Wound, J.D. Isip (2023)
Feed It to the River, Terhi K. Cherry (2022)
Beat Not Beat: An Anthology of California Poets Screwing on the Beat and Post-Beat Tradition (2022)
When There Are Nine: Poems Celebrating the Life and Achievements of Ruth Bader Ginsburg (2022)
The Knife Thrower's Daughter, Terri Niccum (2022)
2 Revere Place, Aruni Wijesinghe (2022)
Here Go the Knives, Kelsey Bryan-Zwick (2022)
Trumpets in the Sky, Jerry Garcia (2022)
Threnody, Donna Hilbert (2022)
A Burning Lake of Paper Suns, Ellen Webre (2021)
Instructions for an Animal Body, Kelly Gray (2021)
Head *V* Heart: New & Selected Poems, Rob Sturma (2021)
Sh!t Men Say to Me: A Poetry Anthology in Response to Toxic Masculinity (2021)
Flower Grand First, Gustavo Hernandez (2021)
Everything is Radiant Between the Hates, Rich Ferguson (2020)
When the Pain Starts: Poetry as Sequential Art, Alan Passman (2020)
This Place Could Be Haunted If I Didn't Believe in Love, Lincoln McElwee (2020)
Impossible Thirst, Kathryn de Lancellotti (2020)

Lullabies for End Times, Jennifer Bradpiece (2020)
Crabgrass World, Robin Axworthy (2020)
Contortionist Tongue, Dania Ayah Alkhouli (2020)
The only thing that makes sense is to grow, Scott Ferry (2020)
Dead Letter Box, Terri Niccum (2019)
Tea and Subtitles: Selected Poems 1999-2019, Michael Miller (2019)
At the Table of the Unknown, Alexandra Umlas (2019)
The Book of Rabbits, Vince Trimboli (2019)
Everything I Write Is a Love Song to the World, David McIntire (2019)
Letters to the Leader, HanaLena Fennel (2019)
Darwin's Garden, Lee Rossi (2019)
Dark Ink: A Poetry Anthology Inspired by Horror (2018)
Drop and Dazzle, Peggy Dobreer (2018)
Junkie Wife, Alexis Rhone Fancher (2018)
The Moon, My Lover, My Mother, & the Dog, Daniel McGinn (2018)
Lullaby of Teeth: An Anthology of Southern California Poetry (2017)
Angels in Seven, Michael Miller (2016)
A Likely Story, Robbi Nester (2014)
Embers on the Stairs, Ruth Bavetta (2014)
The Green of Sunset, John Brantingham (2013)
The Savagery of Bone, Timothy Matthew Perez (2013)
The Silence of Doorways, Sharon Venezio (2013)
Cosmos: An Anthology of Southern California Poetry (2012)
Straws and Shadows, Irena Praitis (2012)
In the Lake of Your Bones, Peggy Dobreer (2012)
I Was Building Up to Something, Susan Davis (2011)
Hopeless Cases, Michael Kramer (2011)
One World, Gail Newman (2011)
What We Ache For, Eric Morago (2010)
Now and Then, Lee Mallory (2009)
Pop Art: An Anthology of Southern California Poetry (2009)
In the Heaven of Never Before, Carine Topal (2008)
A Wild Region, Kate Buckley (2008)
Carving in Bone: An Anthology of Orange County Poetry (2007)
Kindness from a Dark God, Ben Trigg (2007)
A Thin Strand of Lights, Ricki Mandeville (2006)
Sleepyhead Assassins, Mindy Nettifee (2006)
Tide Pools: An Anthology of Orange County Poetry (2006)
Lost American Nights: Lyrics & Poems, Michael Ubaldini (2006)

Patrons

Moon Tide Press would like to thank the following people for their support in helping publish the finest poetry from the Southern California region. To sign up as a patron, visit www.moontidepress.com or send an email to publisher@moontidepress.com.

Anonymous
Robin Axworthy
Conner Brenner
Nicole Connolly
Bill Cushing
Susan Davis
Kristen Baum DeBeasi
Peggy Dobreer
Kate Gale
Dennis Gowans
Alexis Rhone Fancher
HanaLena Fennel
Half Off Books & Brad T. Cox
Donna Hilbert
Jim & Vicky Hoggatt
Michael Kramer
Ron Koertge & Bianca Richards
Gary Jacobelly
Ray & Christi Lacoste

Jeffery Lewis
Zachary & Tammy Locklin
Lincoln McElwee
David McIntire
José Enrique Medina
Michael Miller & Rachanee Srisavasdi
Michelle & Robert Miller
Ronny & Richard Morago
Terri Niccum
Andrew November
Jeremy Ra
Luke & Mia Salazar
Jennifer Smith
Roger Sponder
Andrew Turner
Rex Wilder
Mariano Zaro
Wes Bryan Zwick

Made in the USA
Monee, IL
23 February 2025